MW00810701

LOVE AND SACRIFICE

.

LOVE AND SACRIFICE

·

THE LIFE OF EMMA JUNG

Imelda Gaudissart

Translated from the French by
Kathleen Llanwarne

CHIRON PUBLICATIONS

ASHEVILLE, NORTH CAROLINA

© 2014 by Chiron Publications. All rights reserved. No part of this publication may be reproduced, stored in a retrieval system, or transmitted, in any form by any means, electronic, mechanical, photocopying, recording, or otherwise, without the prior written permission of the publisher, Chiron Publications, 932 Hendersonville Road, Suite 104, Asheville, North Carolina 28803.

Original French edition, *Emma Jung: Analyste et Écrivain*, published by Éditions L'Age d'Homme, Lausanne, Switzerland, 2010.

ISBN 978-1-63051-085-5 paperback
ISBN 978-1-63051-086-2 clothbound

Book and cover design by Marianne Jankowski.
Printed in the United States of America.

Library of Congress Cataloging-in-Publication Data
Gaudissart, Imelda.
    [Emma Jung. English]
    Love and sacrifice : the life of Emma Jung / Imelda Gaudissart; translated from the French by Kathleen Llanwarne.
        pages cm
    Includes bibliographical references and index.
    ISBN 978-1-63051-085-5 (pbk. : alk. paper)
    ISBN 978-1-63051-086-2 (clothbound : alk. paper)
    1. Women psychoanalysts--Switzerland--Biography. 2. Jung, C. G. (Carl Gustav), 1875-1961--Relations with women. 3. Jung, Emma. 4. Jung, C. G. (Carl Gustav), 1875-1961. I. Title.
BF109.J86G38 2014
150.19'54092--dc23
[B]

2014026527

To Pierre, my companion of fifty-six years, and
the precious family we created together

—IG

In memory of my sister-in-translation
Janet Altman (1955–2012) and of
my little brother Nick Llanwarne (1962–2013)

—KL

Anguish and insomnia associated with the creative process are indeed a kind of pleasure . . . a very rare pleasure . . . the challenge of creating some new form of understanding, of revealing perhaps some new aspect of human experience—what could be more exciting?

—JOHN CERULLO, A FRIEND

So my own mind shifts hither and thither wondering if I should stay with my son and keep everything unchanged—my estate, my waiting-women, my lofty-roofed house itself—respecting my husband's bed and the people's voice.

—WORDS SPOKEN BY PENELOPE IN THE ODYSSEY

I make choice of you, to open my heart's griefs to you, and to have your assistance in softening them; you may imagine they are not small; I bear in appearance without much concern the King's engagement with the Duchess of Valentinois, but it is insupportable to me.

—MADAME DE LAFAYETTE, LA PRINCESSE DE CLÈVES

You have to tell them that I suffered deeply.

—EMMA JUNG, IN A TEXT MESSAGE
RECEIVED BY IMELDA IN A DREAM

In my medical experience as well as in my own life I have again and again been faced with the mystery of love, and have never been able to explain what it is. . . . Here is the greatest and smallest, the remotest and nearest, the highest and lowest.

—C. G. JUNG, MEMORIES, DREAMS, REFLECTIONS

CONTENTS

A galllery of photographs follows page 56.

In November 2004, as I was approaching the end of Deirdre Bair's *Jung: A Biography*, a commanding voice called me to attention. The voice said that the time had absolutely come to speak of Emma Jung. Three years passed, during which I mentioned this idea in conversation with friends and family. It was greeted with interest, but also surprise. To most people—with the exception perhaps of Jung's followers—Emma Jung is quite unknown. Finally, in two powerful and symbolic dreams, Emma's presence was expressed. From that point on, my sole task was to respond to her proposal, her request, to be called back from the depths.

This meant setting out on the adventure of an encounter—an encounter with a woman whose story could, quite plausibly, be approached from different angles. The choice that emerged as appropriate is neither history nor fiction. This short book is above all a response to a fundamentally twofold concern: for a spirit of fairness to all parties as well as for the importance of not allowing one woman's primarily inner and hence subjective experience to suffer betrayal. The only reason for setting the story of Emma Jung in a particular social, collective, and cultural context is to enquire into the manner in which she faced her own destiny and to become aware of the remarkable courage she showed in so doing.

from the author

Writing a book is both an individual and a collective creation. If inspiration is the primal source, sharing is nurturing the work. My thanks go first to John Cerullo; by offering me *Jung: A Biography* by Deirdre Bair in 2004, he triggered my curiosity and concern for Emma Jung. To René Stebler, now deceased, who followed me through with passion; he contributed his knowledge of the Swiss traditions and customs. To Helene Hoerni-Jung, a centenarian, who passed away recently and who accepted with grace, to share some of her memories. To Dieter Baumann, Andreas Jung and his wife, Ulrich, and Jost Hoerni, some of the grandchildren, who have been generous opening their door and answering my many questions and requests. To Elizabeth Clark-Stern, who supplied me with the text of her play on Emma and Toni Wolff. To Brigitte Egger, who commented on my manuscript. To Marie Bronchart and Jean-Pierre Delarge for their technical suggestions, and to many others who lie in my heart with emotion and gratitude. To Chiron Publications and the marvelous editing team, which allows Emma Jung to reach the wide Anglo-American public, and to Kathleen Llanwarne for her marvelous translating. Last, but not least, to Emma Jung, who has been the mysterious instigator, staying by my side and ultimately expressing her gratitude. May this story be a tribute to her invaluable contribution to Carl G. Jung's life and work.

from the translator
I would like to thank the following friends, family members, colleagues, and contacts for their many differing forms of practical support, specialist assistance, and encouragement which enabled me to accept Imelda's invitation to produce an English translation of her book on Emma Jung: Mary Brazier, Celia Dixie, Viviane Dunn, Anthony Hirst, Maria Jepsen, Christina Kantarou, Andrew Llanwarne, Nadia Llanwarne, Alec Luyckx, Philippe Pochet, and Anthony Stevens.

1

.

Introduction

The reason for choosing to write about Emma is, clearly, the desire to acknowledge her unique position and the paramount role that she played. Emma Jung is a woman who has moved me to undertake this task. My concern is to do justice to Emma the woman, Emma the wife, Emma the mother, Emma the analyst, and Emma the writer. Emma Jung was a woman who possessed—of this there can be no doubt—the stuff of a heroine.[1]

Factual information included in this book owes much to research conducted by earlier writers deserving of our trust. In elaborating upon the details, I relied on my own discoveries, encounters, and explorations.

To speak of Emma Jung is, in one way, to reverse the established mode of presentation. For this will be a portrait in which, contrary to the usual pecking order, Emma's husband, Carl Gustav Jung, will not be the figure enjoying the limelight.

It is, of course, quite unthinkable to describe Emma's history and personality without Carl Gustav spontaneously entering our thoughts, so closely intertwined are their two lives. Yet it may

---

1. The *Collins Dictionary* definition of *heroine* includes reference to a woman possessed of "superior qualities."

actually be the case that, by focusing our attention on Emma, we become aware of hitherto unnoticed aspects of the personality of C. G. Jung.

To spend fifty-two years of one's life with this towering figure of a man is an exceptional destiny. It is hardly surprising that it has been said of Emma that her marriage with Carl Gustav altered her profoundly. The desire and the need to speak about Emma derive their inspiration from a sense of connection that comes naturally to a woman. She could, after all, have been my own grandmother, and I am moved by this awareness. The rather special circumstances—to say the very least—that marked her life led her to develop a host of qualities that have for too long been left in the shadow.

It seems quite obvious that had Emma not been a person possessed of superior qualities to whom Jung's attention had been spontaneously drawn when she was still very young, she would have been incapable of facing up to and accomplishing such a destiny. It is my firm conviction that it was her strength of character, her intelligence, her natural generosity, and the values she cherished that enabled her to stand up to this challenge and to move through and beyond the trials and suffering she endured. To direct our attention to Emma is to set out in search of suggestive details, as well as evident facts, and to come up with some perhaps bold hypotheses.

It would seem that, a few months before her death, Emma expressed the wish that her correspondents return the letters she had sent them. Was this request prompted by the wish to prevent inappropriate use being made of the traces she left behind? Was it a question of modesty on her part in the face of her husband's position of eminence in the intellectual and cultural world of the time? Today we are in no position to answer this question. Her request was perhaps proof of great wisdom on her part. One of Jung's grandsons contributed the following testimony: "My younger brother, aged fourteen at the time, saw his grandfather burn some letters in the fireplace." Could these have been letters from Emma? Or perhaps from Toni Wolff?

This removal of all traces recalls the striking tradition of the American Indian shamans who draw mandalas in the sand to re-create or express a moment in the harmony of the cosmos. Their duration is ephemeral. The present moment alone has meaning, is alone instilled with value.

It is indeed a highly delicate enterprise—but one that is of the ut-most importance—to attempt to reconstitute the essential elements of Emma's destiny, the ingredients of her history and of her life as she lived it. Over and above the influence still exerted by the work of C. G. Jung, the contribution made by Emma is also of value in today's world. Her story, for this reason, deserves to be told.

The tale will contain some dates because the events recounted belong to a precise period in history. It is sometimes important to assure ourselves of our bearings in this way. The principal protago-nists, Emma and Carl, were affected by the turbulence and tragedy of twentieth-century history. At the same time, they set their own indelible stamp on this history, and these two dimensions exist in a state of subtle coalescence. At other times, it may prove beneficial to be less precise, to inhabit a space where we can allow ourselves to be addressed—and surprised—by our imagination.

Let us begin then at the beginning. Emma Rauschenbach was born on 30 March 1882 and died on 27 November 1955, in her seven-ty-fourth year. Carl Gustav Jung was born on 28 July 1875 and sur-vived his wife by almost six years. He died on 6 June 1961, not long before his eighty-sixth birthday. The age difference between them was thus more than six and a half years, a fact that is not without its importance. We will deliberately recall it from time to time when recounting some of the sequence of specific events that contributed to the fabric of their long lives and all that they shared.

Emma felt a strong need to remain an essentially private and modest person. She disliked honorific titles and was never keen to appear before a camera. For her family, with its bourgeois tradition, the need for discretion was of the utmost concern. And yet Emma found herself present at, and significantly involved in, numerous gatherings and developments in the public and social life of her time. These aspects are to be kept in mind, while remaining aware that the purpose pursued in offering this portrait is neither to provide a factual biography nor to fictionalize Emma's life.

Sixty years have now passed since Emma Jung's death. Any attempt to resuscitate her will inevitably be veiled in a fine mist. With the passage of time, the images and recollections retained in our memories always take on an impressionistic quality. Depending on their age or circumstances, those who knew Emma perceived differing aspects of her personality. A wide range of men and women shared privileged moments with her as wife, mother, grandmother, friend, or therapist. To consider the situation in this way is to perceive the obvious conclusion that even so-called objective events are inevitably shaped and colored by the manner in which they are filtered by our sensitivities, our subjectivities, and our emotional recollection of the past.

Is not our purpose, in seeking to depict a person, to somehow endow with visible features a form of reality that cannot be seen? In two separate dream images that rose up from my unconscious Emma thus acquired representational form. In the first dream she appeared as a magnificent fish emerging into the air out of a well from which I was removing an accumulation of dead leaves and flowers. Jung once referred to fishes in the following way: "And now the magical beauty of the playing fish, colourful, shining, transparent, veiled" (Jung 2008, 356).

The image in the second dream was of a goose with magnificent plumage, exactly as we see such birds represented in the images of ancient Egypt. Seated at a pavement café, I watched it emerge from an underground passage, appearing to be lost and seeking to attract my attention before disappearing once more. I knew intuitively—an understanding confirmed by strong emotion—that the dream image in both cases was Emma Jung. She has continued to accompany me as I write this book.

Why should we not allow ourselves to imagine Emma's personal reactions or even, on occasion, to guess at them? When we begin to travel alongside another being, and even if the journey takes place in complete silence, a subtle sense of fluid connection is established. Such a connection is experienced as surprising, emotionally charged, and, of course, completely subjective. But why should this matter? What is at stake here, surely, is the matter of recalling to awareness a person who has not completely disappeared from the unconscious screens concealed within our psyche or from our collective human experience.

The plan for this portrait fell into shape quite spontaneously. The most natural approach seemed to be to map out the important milestones of Emma's life: birth, upbringing, marriage, family, spheres of involvement, and so forth. And yet the shape of this life is anything but linear. Conditions, encounters, painful episodes and circumstances, and all the innumerable developments thereby entailed, are the threads of which its fabric is woven. In the course of the telling, these threads cross over each other, becoming sometimes entwined and compelled to move forward together. Slowly, through and thanks to the passage of time, this painstaking creation finds its own characteristic form. Indications that lacked substance during the early stages take on meaning and consistency. Like a piece of elaborate needlework that acquires its form so very slowly and gradually, the precise qualities become fully revealed only once it has reached completion.

When one single human being realizes an individual destiny, he or she replays, in a new stage production, a drama springing from sources that have been described in the tragedies and mythologies of humanity. The stage props and the décor change; the order of the scenes will of course vary; minor characters in one version will reappear as central figures in another. Called upon to witness these recurrent themes, we invariably experience deep emotion. Located simultaneously on the stage and among the audience, we are touched by the protagonists' tragedy, which in some of its features coincides with our own.

As a couple, Emma and Carl Gustav Jung were in no way immune to this dynamic. The husband, like Odysseus, was impelled throughout his life to explore the deepest, outermost, and most perilous regions of the human soul. The wife, like Penelope, patiently tended the home, cared for the members of her household, and continued her weaving. These unceasing comings and goings of the two members of a couple are the threads that symbolically serve to relate the long period of waiting, the devotion, the fear, the experiences shared, and the wounds suffered.

These are the elements with which I found myself dealing and which so deeply touched my emotions. From the episodes of Emma's long life there emerges a drama, a web of events and developments, that takes place, above all, on her own inner stage. Reference to the eternal accents of an imaginary odyssey seemed to me an appropriate means of illustrating the complex maze of joys and tears formed by these two destinies; and so, at a number of pertinent points in this story, I draw attention to some of the many parallels between the experiences of its protagonists and the universal template supplied by the Homeric epic and the ancient worldview from which it sprang.

We might begin by imagining the verdict reached by an assembly of the gods convened to rule on the destiny reserved for Carl and Emma:

> To you, Carl Gustav, we open the gates to the deepest
> recesses of the human soul. The price of this journey will
> be your fearsome share of inner peril, and you will leave
> behind you the everlasting record of your voyage.
>
> You, Emma, will weave the rich fabric on which your
> husband's works will be inscribed. Few will know the
> price exacted for the successful performance of this
> lifelong task, marked by all the features of a rich and
> frequently somber tragedy.

And so now you, the reader, are invited to peruse this account of the life of Emma Jung. You may expect to feel, as you go along, reactions of surprise, respect, and admiration. The book sets out to pay tribute and to do justice to a destiny. Its writing was undertaken in response to an inner calling, to a sense of responsibility for a mysterious mission that it fell to me to accomplish. May it have fulfilled its purpose!

2

.

The Girl from Schaffhausen

The town of Schaffhausen is documented as early as 1045 as a city-state that minted its own coinage. Its territory is enclosed within a curve of the Rhine. Initially the town formed part of the Hapsburg Empire. In 1501 it became a member of the Old Swiss Confederacy. Subsequently it developed into the administrative center of what is today a small Swiss canton bordered on three sides by Germany.

Visitors to the old town can admire a number of fine and graciously proportioned Renaissance buildings, their façades decorated with colored frescos and stucco sculptures in a style peculiar to the region. At the end of the nineteenth century this part of the town must have looked much as it still appears today. On account of the world-famous Rhine Falls, the largest waterfall in Europe, located only a short distance from the town, Schaffhausen attracts large numbers of tourists.

The area entered the industrial age in 1857 with the construction of the country's first hydroelectric power station on the Rhine Falls and the laying of a railway line. These developments prompted an American industrialist from Boston named Florentine Ariosto Jones to come to Schaffhausen to seek his fortune. He set up a watchmaking factory in the town in 1868.

Members of the Rauschenbach family had held official positions in Schaffhausen but were known above all for their entrepreneurial skills. In 1880 Johannes Rauschenbach-Vogel bought the watch factory from its founder. The business had at that point gone bankrupt. Thanks to the remarkable talents of four successive generations of the Rauschenbach and Homberger families, the factory was modernized and enlarged, finally becoming the International Watch Company, which was managed as a family business until 1976.

Johannes Rauschenbach-Vogel was Emma Jung's grandfather. He possessed an impressive streak of creative genius, and his name will remain associated above all with the agricultural machinery he invented and which was sold throughout the world. He died in 1881 at age sixty-six, only a year after buying the watch factory, which he had added to his many endeavors. Emma Jung was not to know her paternal grandfather, as she was born on March 30 of the following year.

Johannes's son had been given the same name as his father but in its French form. At the young age of twenty-five, Jean Rauschenbach-Schenk found himself in charge of the family business. And not only was he now a chief company executive, he was also quite recently married. He and his wife, Bertha, moved into the company residence, an attractive house named *Rosengarten* (Rose Garden). In accordance with the custom of the time, this residence had been built close to the industrial estate on the banks of the Rhine. The young couple provided company for Johannes's widow, Maria, who took some consolation in their presence. She enjoyed whiling away the hours with her two small granddaughters, Emma and Marguerite, with whom she shared her collections of dolls. The two little girls were also frequently spellbound by their grandmother's tales of ghosts.

It is important to realize that Emma was born into a family that was not of the nobility but rather owed its access to high society to its recently acquired industrial fortune. In a small Swiss town the rise of this new and exceedingly dynamic class of bourgeois industrialists caused more than a few ripples within the patrician society with its staid, traditional ways. As time went on, the contrast between the two groups altered the appearance and character of the town of Schaffhausen quite considerably. Apart from their strictly industrial responsibilities, the men of Emma's family had always shown concern for the social and material condition of the men and women employed by the family business. Their attitude in this respect might be described, in contemporary parlance, as enlightened paternalism.

Emma grew up in an atmosphere that was luxurious but at the same time sober, imbued with social, moral, and religious principles. She would later reminisce about her childhood spent in the family residences, endowing this period with a magical quality. The most important figures during the two sisters' childhood years spent at Rosengarten were their paternal grandmother, Maria Rauschenbach-Vogel, and their mother, Bertha. The general atmosphere of the home environment was predominantly feminine.

The life of these bourgeois industrialists had its own specific rhythm and features. They lived very close to their business activities, surrounded by the factory buildings. The owner was never out of sight of the workers' movements or out of hearing of the noisy machinery. The adults gave receptions; friends and family came to visit. The horses would be harnessed or the motorcar taken out for excursions or longer journeys. All these arrangements together represented a microcosm of a new and flourishing social class, governed by its own particular rules and traditions.

In addition to the presence of their grandmother and mother, the two little girls were surrounded by the domestic staff that formed part of the household. Emma and her sister attended a public school reserved principally for the social elite of the town, in addition to which they had a private tutor at home. Nor was there any shortage of learning facilities and opportunities in the family library. In this manner, Emma continued her schooling up to the age of fifteen or sixteen.

By the mid-1890s, Emma's father had become an extremely wealthy industrialist. Still quite young, he was already suffering from a host of physical complaints, although nothing certain has been established about their origins. It is known, at any rate, that he became partially blind. In spite of his poor health, he decided to purchase a large and partially derelict property.

The location of the new property was undoubtedly somewhere quite out of the ordinary. *Ölberg* (Mount Olive) was on a hillside just outside the town. In addition to the existing house, there was a late Romanesque chapel, which had contained a series of sculptures representing Christ's Passion, but the Protestant Reformation had left it in ruins. On the surrounding hillside a gallows and beheading block had been constructed. Jean Rauschenbach had the house demolished so as to build an extremely spacious new residence in its place. Emma and Marguerite, who expressed a liking for the old stones, protested to no avail. However, their father preserved the place name Ölberg.

Keen no doubt to provide public evidence of his wealth and social position, he decided, together with an architect, to build an impressive house in a somewhat rococo composite style with an abundance of balconies, spires, and loggias. The interior was richly designed, incorporating different art nouveau trends of the period. Oak was the predominant material used, visible in the extensive wall paneling as well as in the imposing staircases and coffered ceilings. Such splendid decorative woodwork and the spacious central hall, which could be opened up to a series of elegant reception rooms, are reminiscent of a bygone age.

In the course of this project, Jean took comfort in being able to rely for assistance on his teenage daughter, Emma. Her concern for her father meant she was happy to help and to discuss not just the building work but also the state of his health; she also, on occasion, read aloud to him. It was an experience that matured the girl beyond her years, and she became accustomed to dealing with a wide range of adult concerns. She avidly read the books she chose for her father, and while her own preferences tended toward the literary, she was also interested in scientific matters. Industrial processes were part of her environment and her native curiosity embraced this subject too.

So it was that Emma and her sister made the transition to adulthood in the new family residence. They settled comfortably on a floor of the new house reserved especially for them, arranging and decorating their rooms according to their taste, taking pleasure in the choice of bedding fabrics, china, color schemes, and wall coverings, yet discovering that their individual tastes and preferences were often dissimilar. They were allowed to indulge their fantasy, and the two sisters, only eighteen months apart in age, were extremely close. Having shared so much enthusiasm and frequent laughter during their adolescent years, they subsequently remained united by a strong lifelong tie.

While the affection that bound the sisters to one another was never called into question, their respective characters and personalities were radically opposed. Emma was perceived to be a decidedly shy child, and this tendency toward reserve remained as she grew up. With her introverted personality, she displayed very early on a bent for books and study.[2] Marguerite had an artistic disposition, enjoyed sport, and was decidedly extraverted in temperament. These differences and complementary character traits certainly caused the occasional friction between the sisters, but without ever jeopardizing the depth of their feelings for one another.

Of a naturally serious disposition, Emma was endowed with a fine intelligence that she channeled into an interest in both natural science and philosophy. At the age of sixteen, after brilliantly completing her schooling, Emma may well have expressed the desire to continue her studies, but this was a direction in which her father, himself self-taught, gave her no encouragement. At the end of the nineteenth century, the Swiss universities, although they occasionally accepted women students from other countries, were not open to female students from Switzerland itself. What is more, the fact of

---

2. Jung was to confirm subsequently that his wife's psychological type was introverted sensation.

belonging to a privileged social class entailed a number of principles and had its disadvantages. Was it not the main priority for a girl of this class, during this period, to learn the skills required to run a household and prepare herself for marriage to a worthy suitor from a similar social background?

To help Emma get over her disappointment, her parents had the idea of letting her spend a few months in France. Some close friends, belonging to the wealthy and cultured ranks of Parisian society, welcomed her into their home, offering her a first taste of the life of the refined French bourgeoisie, in exchange for some help on Emma's part in caring for their young children. These people were highly cultured, traveled long distances to take family holidays, invited guests to their home, and held parties. This was indeed a fine opportunity for a young girl so full of curiosity and with a true thirst for learning. Emma was able, under these circumstances, to gain an entry into a different, fascinating, and highly stimulating world.

We can imagine how excited she must have found it to be living in Paris, where countless opportunities were available for her to further her education. Here she was in contact with a truly cosmopolitan world. She learned to speak French with relative ease, took advantage of the numerous museums and art galleries, and enjoyed the heady atmosphere of a capital city. It may well be that her discovery of and interest in the legend of the Holy Grail dates from this period through the works in Old French of Chrétien de Troyes. Emma's encounter with this tale was, in any case, an experience that never left her, and the effort to compose a work that explored the rich and multifaceted symbolism and psychology of this legend was to constitute a major lifelong project.

On her return to Schaffhausen Emma was seventeen years old and had quite obviously derived tremendous benefit from this exceptional social and cultural experience. Before the young woman's gaze Paris had opened up a window through which the city's treasures had entered her mind. Her stay in France had enabled her to leave behind, for a period, her home town and family milieu and to breathe a different air. On returning to Schaffhausen she was full of joy and keen to share her discoveries with her family members.

From time to time Emma, together with her friends, reveled in the heady delights of dancing parties. These soirées were reserved for young people of a select class, with attendance subject to personal invitation. Parents did not fail to encourage advantageous matches among their sons and daughters on these occasions, and Emma was, beyond any doubt, a young lady much in demand. Renewing our earlier parallel with the universal accents of ancient Greek epic and the worldview to which it gives expression, we might imagine that the women of the chorus, if invited to attend these romantic occasions and partake of their pleasures, would have drawn our attention to their ephemeral nature and whispered in Emma's ear:

> Live to the full your splendid youth, pretty flower. This
> short-lived time of life, with its subtle and sometimes
> forbidden pleasures, will slip through your fingers, leaving
> an indelible but ineffable trace in your heart.

A new century was about to dawn. The year was 1899, and a chapter in Emma's existence—quite unbeknown to the young girl herself—was about to end in a most unexpected manner: Carl Gustav Jung was soon to enter her life, nevermore to leave it.

Carl G. Jung was later to say, curiously, that he had known Emma for a very long time. The two mothers, Emilie Jung and Bertha Schenk, had been close friends for many years. They had been members of the same parish, the pastor of which was none other than Paul Jung, Carl's father. Carl remembered that, as a child, he had been on walks along the banks of the Rhine with his mother and in the company of a pretty young blond woman. This was Bertha, who had married into the Rauschenbach family, and the elder of the two little girls who were with her on these occasions was Emma.

Carl also related that at the age of seventeen, as a guest of the Rauschenbach family, he had espied at the top of the fine staircase in the house called Rosengarten a little girl of eleven who appeared rather shy. He believed he was seeing a young princess. The child, of course, was Emma, and the penetrating glance from her fine blue eyes made the girl appear older than her years. The seventeen-year-old boy had been transfixed by the sight of her, even though she had come into view for no more than a moment. In a photo taken around this time, Emma can be seen wearing an elegant high-necked dress, in keeping with the fashion of the period.

A few years later, on the occasion of another invitation from Frau Rauschenbach, Carl once again set eyes upon Emma. At the time he was twenty-one, a student in Basel living on very little money. The young man's penury, quite obvious from the state of his clothes, was in striking contrast to his family's rich intellectual heritage. Emma was fourteen, and by this time her family had moved to the new house at Ölberg. To the astonishment of those to whom he later confessed this fact, Jung said that he had known on this occasion, with absolute certainty, that Emma would become his wife. What audacity on his part, one might be tempted to think, since in terms of their social status—and in spite of the fact that Carl's ancestry included a number of intellectually brilliant figures—the two of them stood far apart. Nor was there any indication whatsoever that the young girl's family might ever consent to such a surprising match.

We are naturally free to fantasize about this moment, to imagine what might have passed through the young man's heart and mind. What was it about Emma that had bowled him over in this way? Was it the impression of her discretion, the peace and calm that emanated from her presence? Was it her already serenely established personality, her quiet self-assurance, her natural charm? Attraction and fascination rise up from the unconscious. The emotion triggered by such an unexpected encounter may confuse the rational mind. It strikes a chord which surges from an unknown depth. Emotions of this kind can dazzle us to the point of blindness, and Carl Gustav Jung fell under just such a spell.

The years passed. Emma spent her year in Paris. Carl finished his studies and was preparing to leave Basel. He had greatly appreciated the open and stimulating atmosphere of this renowned university, but the actual city of Basel was a little too small to his taste. He was accepted as a trainee psychiatrist in the relatively new Burghölzli public hospital located just outside Zürich, which was already an establishment of considerable repute. From time to time he continued to receive invitations to Ölberg, which he did not hesitate to accept. Such trips into the country made a change from his studious and rather austere life as a resident house officer in psychiatry.

Imagine overhearing the musings of the gods on Mount Olympus at this point in the tale: Will Carl Gustav, this young man so enamored of life and so much under the spell of his attraction to Emma, be capable of reining in the wild and impulsive side of his own nature sufficiently to win the heart of this pretty and discreet young lady with her refined upper-class tastes? Does not the decision rest with Emma herself? Will she be prepared to exchange her refined and cosseted existence to embark on a life of adventure with this unusual and rather strange young man?

And could these gods, as they indulge in their curious gossip, feign to ignore that Emma, in moving away from the whirlpool of industrial pioneers in which she grew up, would be choosing a path through life within another equally vibrant microcosmic sphere that was just beginning to be forged by the pioneers of the human soul?

In a rather subtle manner that was characteristic of the period, it was Bertha who guided her daughter's choice in marriage. She finally succeeded in winning over her husband who initially had not been in the least keen on the idea of Carl courting his daughter. Emma herself was somewhat hesitant. In her own mind she was already destined to become engaged to a young local man, a member of "a good Schaffhausen family." Possibly she simply did not yet feel ready, or perhaps she was somewhat afraid of this rather strange suitor so unlike most of the young men who had peopled her immediate world to date.

However, Carl Gustav's feelings of love and attraction toward the young woman were commensurate with his impassioned and impetuous temperament. He saw to it that, thanks to his keen insistence, the last vestiges of resistance gradually melted away. It is not difficult to imagine Carl, whether living in Zürich or in Paris, baring his soul through his pen and sending Emma furiously passionate letters in which he declared his love and shared with her the fruits of his research, his discoveries, and his doubts. Emma genuinely admired the young man's personality, his tremendously wide-ranging culture and intelligence. She indeed found him to be quite different from all the other men she had met so far. What is more, she trusted her mother's intuition.

And so events moved quickly. Emma would soon be twenty and Carl was already twenty-seven. He was continuing his stint as psychiatrist-in-training at the Burghölzli hospital. The engagement was officially announced in October 1901. In the autumn of 1902 Jung, encouraged by his supervisor, Professor Eugen Bleuler, went to Paris to work under Pierre Janet, the head of psychiatry at the Salpêtrière hospital, where he spent six months.

The wedding took place in February 1903. A religious ceremony was held at the Schaffhausen Reformed Church, to which the family belonged. Two days later, on February 16, family and friends were invited to a banquet. The newlywed couple, in company with their many guests, enjoyed a festive twelve-course menu accompanied by a selection of the best wines. Family members remember tales of the couple's honeymoon, spent first by Lake Como and traveling from there to the Canary Islands. The honeymoon trip had been paid for by Emma's parents, a gift that was part of her dowry. Carl, whose means were quite modest in comparison, must have felt like the happiest and most fortunate man on earth. The wonders of the southern island scenery and sights, in conjunction with their happiness as newlyweds, likely dazzled the young couple and appeared as a fitting mode of inaugurating their new life and the joys to come. Carl, considering the matter in his own mind, could feel a legitimate sense of pride at having gained entry to this wealthy family. While giving praise for his good luck, he was entitled to feel that his own value, his wide-ranging culture, and his tremendous ambition represented an equally precious gift for his young wife Emma.

3

.

The Burghölzli Years

The girl from Schaffhausen had become Emma Jung, whose destiny
as a married woman was to prove rich in manifold developments.
Yet for the time being she was quite simply a woman in love, and
her only regret on moving away from her home town following her
marriage was that she was leaving an ailing father behind her. This
sorrow was tempered perhaps somewhat by the exciting prospect of
living in Zürich.

In comparison with Schaffhausen, Zürich had the definite air of
a capital city. Located on the edge of the lake of the same name, it
is a city surrounded by a forested landscape with mountains of me-
dium height. By the beginning of the twentieth century—the period
we have now reached in our account of Emma's life— Zürich had
become a hub that attracted not only industry and trade but also
culture. Its university was well known, and several famous writers,
including Thomas Mann, James Joyce, and Hermann Hesse, became
associated with the city and left a permanent mark on it. Emma and
Carl Jung were to meet these great figures and others on a number
of occasions.

At the very beginning of their married life, after a brief stay
in an apartment in Zurich Center, Carl and Emma Jung had no

option but to move into the Burghölzli, the psychiatric hospital where Carl had now been appointed to a post of medical officer. The rule that doctors at the Burghölzli take up their living quarters within the hospital premises was, at that time, a condition of their employment. Signifying, as it did, a strict level of discipline at all times, such an arrangement entailed a number of constraints. It meant, for instance, that they were neighbors with Carl's immediate superior, Professor Eugen Bleuler, and with the other resident doctors. In any case, the young couple was allocated a rather spacious apartment equipped with a decent level of modern comfort.

Whether Emma had been given the opportunity to visit the premises before consenting to marry Carl seems not to be on record. We can imagine that Emma's heart must have sunk as she climbed the two majestic flights of stairs leading up to their apartment. Here Emma was inside a mental hospital, where she had agreed to make her home so as to follow her husband. Echoing through the corridor, the psychiatric patients' groans and wails could sometimes be heard coming from behind closed doors. She was pleased to discover at least that their apartment, situated on the second floor, had a view over the gardens, vineyards, and woods surrounding the hospital premises, which were located in the countryside some five miles away from Zurich.

It certainly cannot have been easy for Emma to make this move and adapt to the contrast between her new home and the large and tasteful Ölberg residence she had left behind in Schaffhausen. She was, and with good reason, fearful of losing her freedom and her independence. The opportunity to furnish and decorate to her own taste this new dwelling located within the austere hospital premises could hardly be said to constitute a luxury. She did, however, succeed in making the rooms elegant, thanks to the classic and high-quality furniture she had brought from Schaffhausen. In accordance with the traditions of the time and the magnitude of the Rauschenbach family fortune, Emma had received a generous dowry. She had been able to select expensive items with which to furnish and decorate her new home. She was no doubt advised and aided by her mother and perhaps also by her grandmother, and her choices, while refined, were never ostentatious. This preference was a reflection of her character and personality as well as of the family tradition.

For Professor Bleuler, who lived with his family on the floor below the Jungs, this living environment represented the expression of a fundamental and deeply espoused vocation. His origins were, in any case, substantially more modest, and he lacked the wealth that Carl, thanks to Emma's moneyed background, was now able to enjoy. The fact that families so different from one another were required to live in such close proximity inevitably focused attention on these cultural and social differences and inequalities. It was a potentially brittle situation which, in the interest of peaceable and pleasant coexistence, called for a degree of tact and goodwill on both sides. Jung respected Bleuler—to whom we owe the term *schizophrenia*—and regarded him with affection. At the same time, however, he was rapidly, if surreptitiously, gaining a degree of ascendancy over his director.

All these factors tended to set the couple apart from their neighbors and inclined them initially to keep social contacts to a minimum. Carl and Emma preferred to dine in town, for both had a gourmet streak and enjoyed fine restaurants and haute cuisine. They found time also to attend cultural events. Zürich had an opera house and a famous symphony orchestra. There was, in other words, no shortage of entertainment. The pleasures of this first year in Zürich were very much those of a happy extended honeymoon period.

Carl's time was, of course, largely taken up by his professional concerns but, living some distance from the city center, he and Emma were able to take advantage of their leisure to enjoy the delights of the surrounding countryside during the hours of freedom from professional duties. The presence of water and mountains was important for Carl's sense of personal balance. A man of tremendous energy, he encouraged his wife to share in his passion for sailing and excursions into the mountains. Though Emma did not have the same fearless enthusiasm and sporting disposition, it would not have been easy for her to turn down Carl's suggestions in this respect. What is more, it is quite likely that she derived pleasure and indeed a sense of comfort and security from her husband's robust health and spirit of adventure, particularly in that it was in such striking contrast to her father's sickly disposition.

Emma's ties with her family remained strong and close. Her parents and sometimes her sister would appear in Zürich on frequent visits, and Emma returned to Ölberg often, for Jean Rauschenbach's state of health was deteriorating rapidly. This situation was a source of great concern to Emma, who still had close emotional ties with her highly intelligent and sensitive father. Fortunately, Schaffhausen and Zürich were only about fifty kilometers apart and were connected by a railway line. For Emma's parents a visit to their married daughter was an opportunity for an outing, either in their chauffeur-driven car or personal horse-driven carriage.

As Emma did not have her own transport, she would sometimes take advantage of these parental visits or use public transportation to go into Zürich to explore what the city had to offer. Thanks to the presence in the household of a domestic servant, she was not required to spend much of her time on housework, for which indeed she had little taste or inclination. Instead, she devoted her available time to cultivating her mind. She embarked, for instance, on a project to research the Holy Grail, and Zürich had a splendid public library that proved a valuable asset in this work.

In the institutional atmosphere of the Burghölzli, Emma displayed considerable diplomacy, using her natural charm, kind disposition, and customary tact to temper any sign of conflict and to relieve the tensions inherent in this excessively regulated hospital environment. As a result of her refined upbringing and respectful nature, Emma gained the affection of all. She even ended up becoming the confidante of numerous members of the hospital staff. Having to work and live some distance from the city, enclosed within the hospital confines, the nursing staff's complaints related above all to the excessively strict institutional discipline and the austere atmosphere, which Emma too was affected by in so many aspects of her daily life. She was unable to feign indifference to the anguish that sometimes afflicted the Burghölzli staff. In the same spirit of spontaneous sympathy, she maintained affectionate relations with the Bleuler family and, in particular, with their teenage children. Living just downstairs, these young people became frequent visitors after the birth of Carl and Emma's own children, for they clearly enjoyed the company of this charming young mother with her welcoming smiles.

The proximity between their private apartment and Carl's workplace also had the effect of bringing Emma into close contact with her husband's professional activities and concerns. She became his assistant, his secretary, his coworker. She helped him write up clinical reports and, above all, acted as his research assistant. Carl's research at this time derived its substance from his daily observation of the multifaceted manifestations of mental illness, especially psychosis. Jung was a relative novice in this field, but he threw himself with passionate commitment into discovering the wide-ranging pathological phenomena displayed by his patients.

These daily contacts with severely pathological cases enabled Jung to gain access to unknown or uncharted regions of the human psyche. The images described by his patients, the accounts they supplied of their experiences, sometimes bore uncanny similarities to religious stories or myths. Could it be that the unconscious was a reservoir of contents shared by humanity as a whole? Jung's first book, *The Psychology of Dementia Praecox*, which dates from his years at the Burghölzli, set out his initial hypotheses concerning the possible existence of a collective unconscious and its archetypal contents. Emma was present and followed this book as it was in the making.

Jung was also, at this time, working on a word association test that he devised with his colleague and friend Ludwig Binswanger

and with Franz Riklin.[3] Emma, out of interest and curiosity, agreed
to undergo this test, and Carl likewise served as a subject for Binswanger. All were deeply struck by how much these tests revealed
of the movements of the unconscious psyche. Jung, regarding the
test as a valuable tool for diagnosis, presented it in public. He even
sent it to Freud. On account of this test and its potential for aiding
diagnosis, Jung earned considerable fame, and though he himself
subsequently abandoned it, the test remains in use today.

Emma was involved also in the work of research and documen-
tation for the book *Symbols of Transformation*, which first appeared
in 1912. This work was to be decisive for Jung's own development
but, at the same time, was to seriously damage his relationship with
Freud. Emma, as a result of her involvement, was subsequently competent to discuss the issues raised in this work with Freud in a letter
she wrote to him. That Emma, in spite of the increasing demands
imposed by motherhood and a growing family, should have become
so familiar with her husband's work is revealing of her personality
and of her innate need for the ongoing stimulation provided by
new learning. Her capacity for grasping the constant flow of new
hypotheses that sprung from Jung's mind is the impressive manifestation of a natural intellectual curiosity.

It is abundantly evident that Emma took a deep and avid interest in these exchanges with her husband and her involvement in his
work. These were pursuits that enriched her mind while stimulating
and satisfying her curiosity. Carl, for whom these areas of inquiry
were of passionate interest and concern, was delighted to share his
hypotheses and discoveries with his wife, who was so deeply receptive to these questions. The issues at stake indeed converged in many

---

3. The test procedure involves presenting a subject with a list of words. These are spoken one at a time, and after hearing each word the subject is asked to give a synonym or
an association. The words are taken from everyday language. A significant delay between
the speaking of the word and the subject's reaction or the manifestation of strong emotion were evidence, in Jung's view, that a fundamental emotion had been triggered. This
emotion pointed to the existence of an unconscious complex that had been aroused by
the procedure, a complex being an autonomous part of the psyche that functions beyond
the control of consciousness.

respects with the subjects of Emma's own research and the questions raised in her mind by the mysterious tales and offshoots of the Grail legend. Her deep fascination with the underlying symbolic dimension of this body of work was a preoccupation that never left her. For the young couple these were precious moments of close contact that were fueled by their shared—and active sharing of—intellectual interests. In this way, their feelings of respect and growing love for one another put down deeper roots. What is more, the contrasting austerity of their surroundings had the effect of further enhancing these moments of grace. Such interludes of deep, shared feeling and enthusiasm may appear, with hindsight, as though surrounded by a halo of dazzling colors, as representing a bright interval of sunshine, magnificent but all too short-lived, in a sky that was rapidly filling with dark and menacing clouds.

Jung even embarked, briefly, on an analysis of his wife. To undertake such an enterprise is now considered quite obviously unacceptable, but at the time it was not uncommon. The newly forming field of psychoanalysis constituted a small world, and there was a shortage of trained professionals. Since a stance of respectful neutrality was impossible in such cases, objectivity could be no more than a matter of lip service, and the results, from the analysand's subjective standpoint, were bound to be unsatisfactory. The experiment was, in any case, to be of very short duration because Jung himself became rapidly aware of the impossibility of retaining a "respectful distance." This was a difficulty to which he subsequently referred in a letter to Freud: "Analysis of one's spouse is one of the more difficult things, unless mutual freedom is assured. The prerequisite for a good marriage, it seems to me, is the license to be unfaithful" (McGuire 1974, 175J).[4]

4. The correspondence between Freud and Jung was first published in English under the editorship of William McGuire in 1974 (for full details see list of references). An abridged version followed in 1979. The same system for numbering the letters is used in both volumes and given here instead of the usual page numbers. Thus 175J is letter no. 175 from Jung to Freud, while numbers followed by F refer to letters from Freud to Jung. Also included in the collection are a few letters from Emma to Freud and some of his replies. Emma's letters are not numbered and will be cited using the initials EJ followed by the date of the letter.

Emma, fortunately, subsequently had the benefit of another analytical relationship with Leonhard Seif. A neurologist trained in Munich, Dr. Seif had become interested in investigating the neuroses that he detected behind the manifestation of neurological disorders. He was a man appreciated for his humanity, and he had come to Zürich in order to take lessons from Jung in the practice of psychotherapy. While Emma was not suffering from any particular disorder of the psyche, her life in this psychiatric hospital environment was far from easy. Furthermore, her husband's personality sometimes constituted a source of considerable perplexity for Emma. The presence of Dr. Seif represented an opportunity for her to find, in an analytical setting, a listener whose approach would be respectful and, above all, more objective than that of her husband.

Toward the end of 1903 Emma's sister, Marguerite, married Ernst Jakob Homberger. Marguerite had recently turned twenty. Ernst, fourteen years older than his young wife, was described as a discreet, wise, and caring man and possessing impressive business acumen. Their wedding was arranged somewhat hurriedly on account of the deteriorating state of health of the bride's father. Given the circumstances, and unlike the large wedding reception that had been held for Emma and Carl at the beginning of the same year, Marguerite and Ernst's marriage ceremony was a much quieter affair.

The young Homberger couple went initially to live at Ölberg. They were company for Bertha and assisted in the care of her sick husband. They naturally also derived pleasure and enjoyment from the spacious building and beautiful environment. Before long, however, keen to preserve the intimacy of a rapidly growing family, the couple decided to build a fine residence of their own, one that would adequately reflect their affluence and aspirations.[5]

While on the subject of Marguerite, it may be worth also mentioning that her visits to Emma at the Burghölzli created something

5. The house, excessively large and ill suited to the realities and domestic constraints of modern life, was sold after Marguerite's death in the early 1970s. Ölberg, on the other hand, remains to this day the home of the Homberger-Rauschenbach descendants.

of a stir. She would arrive—as the gossip columns of the day reveled in pointing out—sporting the latest fashions and at the wheel of her own car. The flamboyant lifestyle of her newly married sister was in stark contrast at that time to Emma's own circumstances, obliged as she was to set up a home in a much more modest and institutional dwelling. The discreet and tactful attitude adopted by Emma so as not to shock persons in her immediate environment contrasted glaringly with her sister's situation and behavior. Did Marguerite realize how much courage was required for Emma to go about her daily life with a smile on her face within these gloomy institutionalized walls?

Meanwhile, even Carl, whose salary was still that of a relatively junior hospital doctor, was not without a tendency to feel hard done by in the face of these differences at the level of social appearances and material comfort. While he certainly never regretted his choice of medicine as a profession, Jung could not completely disguise some twinges of envy on seeing his brother-in-law Ernst free to travel when and where he wished, even if his journeys were more often than not for business.

The following year, 1904, was an eventful one. In the spring Emma became aware that she was pregnant. Carl and Emma's first child, a daughter, Agathe, was born on December 26. Emma, having become a mother at the age of twenty-two, embarked joyfully on her new role in life under the tender gaze of Carl and the enlightened ministrations of her mother, Bertha. The arrival of motherhood prompted the beginnings of a gradual change in the relationship between Emma and Carl in a manner that was at first very subtle. Jung was powerfully focused on and preoccupied by his career. His ambition was tremendous, his skills abundantly apparent, and his intuitions constantly on the alert. Emma, bringing into play her maturity and natural talent for fostering harmony in relationships, did her utmost to maintain balance within her marriage while tending to the needs of a growing family and, at the same time, ministering to those of her own and Carl's families of origin.

Carl's sphere of activity was widening all the time. By now, encouraged initially by Professor Bleuler and inspired subsequently by his meeting with Freud, he was seeing increasing numbers of men and women who had been personally recommended to him for private analytical treatment, his reputation having spread far beyond the walls of the Burghölzli. One such patient was Sabina Spielrein, who had come all the way from Russia. She was nineteen when she began her treatment with Jung in August 1904. Here we will say no more than that it was the arrival of this young patient—who was to cause many tongues to wag and a great deal of ink to flow—that occasioned the first serious emotional disruption in the life of the married couple. The repercussions of Sabina's presence in their social environment and the turbulence that overflowed into the still small world constituted by the nascent practice of psychoanalysis, were indeed to take them quite by surprise.

The year 1905 began sorrowfully. In March Jean Rauschenbach died at the early age of forty-eight, leaving behind a great fortune and a grieving and bewildered family. Bertha and his two daughters inherited a large and important watch factory. His son-in-law, Ernst J. Homberger, took over the reins of the family firm, which he would enlarge still further and cause to prosper during the forty years he spent at its head.

Carl, in his capacity as head of household and in accordance with the laws of Switzerland at the time, became legally responsible for managing Emma's share of the inheritance. While ostentation was quite foreign to both of them, there can be no denying that the couple gained tremendous freedom from this sudden state of affluence. The inheritance was to enable Carl, throughout his life, to conduct his research and to travel as he wished. Emma, meanwhile, perceived that she would now have the opportunity to set their family life on a secure and prosperous footing, quite free of material care.

The family was not slow in taking shape. A second daughter, Gret, was born in February 1906. The age difference between Emma and Carl's first two daughters was practically the same as that separating Emma and her own sister. The next child to arrive was Franz, the eagerly awaited son, who was born in 1908. Marianne was the fourth child, born in 1910, and Helene (known as Lill)—a ravishingly beautiful child, it was said—was the couple's last child, born in 1914.

Was each of these pregnancies welcome? This is a matter over which Emma herself drew a veil of discretion. While the birth of a child is cause for great joy, it inevitably also entails prolonged fatigue and innumerable sources of worry. In Emma's life, the experience of successive childbearing undoubtedly represents a burden that cannot be ignored. She must have suffered at times from loneliness and isolation in the course of these first years of marriage spent in a fortress that had been built to shelter the victims of insanity and which, out of love of life and family, she lit up and animated with her smile.

Carl's perception of a life spent largely confined within this closed asylum was quite different, for his tremendous enthusiasm and creativity had the power to burst open its walls. It is possible— who can say?—that he was nonetheless aware of the constraining situation he was imposing on his wife. While he asserted that Emma consented to these successive pregnancies (see Carotenuto 1977), it is legitimate to wonder about the hidden or complex underpinnings of this acceptance.

The years spent at the Burghölzli came to an end in 1909. Jung's professional situation had developed and changed considerably. His international reputation was growing all the time, and he wished from now on to chart his own path. Emma found the apartment simply too small to contain her growing family. After a careful search, the family acquired a piece of land on the shores of Lake Zürich at Küsnacht, which at the time was a quiet village some seven kilometers outside Zürich.

In this way Carl and Emma were able finally to realize their cherished dream: a home of their own by the lakeside. The house was designed by Carl—with the aid of a cousin, an architect by profession—but the money behind the venture was from Emma's inheri-

tance. Their son, Franz, who became an architect and subsequently
inherited the house, was to say of it that it was exceptional in no
respect other than its size. According to Franz, the most architectur-
ally pleasing part of the building was his father's quarters on the first
floor.[6] Here, in the central area of the house, Jung set up his office
and his library overlooking the lake.

Emma's childhood and youth had been spent in great mansions.
Now, having become accustomed to more modest surroundings,
while yet delighted at the change, she felt almost ashamed to enter
such a huge house, so glaring was the contrast with the Burghölzli
apartment in which she had spent her married life so far. Presum-
ably, the fact that many other large properties on the lakeside were
on a par with the new residence must have gone some way in helping
Emma get over this initial sense of disorientation.

The property included a fine area of parkland some distance
from the road and with direct access to the lake. The children soon
became accustomed to living close to the water; the lapping of the
waves could be heard from the house together with the rolling
sound made by pebbles on the shore as they softly shifted position
under the incessant movement of the rippling water. As soon as he
moved into the new house, Jung began receiving his professional cli-
ents there. His library, over the years, was to be constantly enriched
with countless volumes that served to inspire and to document his
studies, research, and writings. The family, thanks to this move to
Küsnacht, now felt free to take in a deep new breath of fresh air.

On an engraved stone, subsequently built into the outer wall of
the house, we can read in German:

Jung waren wir	Young we were
Jung hiessen wir	And Young was our name
Der ewigen Jugend	Eternal youth
Gehören wir	is where we belong

6. These quarters were on the floor above the ground floor, what Americans would call
the second floor.

This engraved quotation expressed quite unequivocally the deep joy that must have filled Emma's and Carl's hearts and spirits on moving into their new residence, their long and ardently desired house by the lake.

4

.

Emma's Relationships with Freud, Jung, and Sabina Spielrein

The last two years of Emma and Carl's residence at the Burghölzli coincided with the first encounter and beginning of the friendship between Carl Gustav Jung and Sigmund Freud. The historic first meeting between the two men took place in Vienna on Sunday, March 3, 1907.

This encounter, which was to lead to highly noteworthy progress in the understanding and practice of psychoanalysis, was, of course, of paramount importance for Jung, but no less so for Emma. The reason for including this chapter in an account of Emma is that she was very much caught up and directly involved in these years of meetings and separation, friendship, admiration, mutual trust, and, finally, dramatic breakup. At a time when women were very rarely represented in the world of professional psychoanalysis, Emma was one of the few women to be invited—in her capacity as Jung's co-worker—to the International Psychoanalytic Congress, held in Weimar in 1911. It is a remarkable fact that Emma should have so naturally succeeded in winning a place in this almost exclusively male world, this fast developing and highly effervescent new scientific community.

During a relatively brief and yet crucial period, several new relationships were born and developed concurrently, at the center of which was the relationship between Jung and Freud. Emma, at the same time, became friendly with Martha Freud while also developing a touchingly close friendship with Freud himself. Additionally, there was Sabina Spielrein, whose arrival and the chaotic sequence of events that followed in its wake marked these few years as a period of painful uncertainty, passion, and adventure. In the context of these encounters and their complex developments and repercussions, the relationship between Carl Gustav and Emma was put to the test and was to undergo deep change.

Professor Sigmund Freud was far from a stranger to Carl. Born in May 1856, he was Jung's elder by nineteen years. Freud's training was in clinical neurology, and he had spent a year working in Paris under the famous neurologist of the time, Jean-Martin Charcot, before moving to Vienna, where he worked closely with Josef Breuer, the "grandfather of psychoanalysis." Freud had gone on to gain recognition as the first doctor and writer to describe the unconscious phenomena associated with hysteria. Following Charcot, Freud had initially proposed hypnosis as a form of treatment, but subsequently abandoned this approach. He had already published several works, of which *The Interpretation of Dreams* and *Three Essays on Sexuality* were particularly noteworthy. Born in Moravia of Jewish parentage he was now, at the time when Jung met him, living in Vienna, married, and the father of five growing children age twelve to twenty. Such are the salient facts about the man whose scientific approach and remarkable personal qualities were to mark Jung's own life and thought so deeply and enduringly.

As early as 1900, Jung had known of Freud's positions on problems relating to psychopathology and possible methods of treatment. Nor was Freud uninformed about the existence of the Burghölzli hospital, and his opinion of what went on there was, by and large, rather favorable. In the years immediately preceding the meeting between the two men, a kind of ritualized to-ing and fro-ing of communications took place between the young Swiss psychiatrist and the Viennese pundit who had already become, within a limited circle, the beneficiary of unquestioning reverence in recognition of his pioneering achievements. The relationship had begun with an exchange of articles and some rather formal letters that served as emissaries for the supply of information on the respective positions of the two professionals. Freud and Jung were taking the measure of one another and of the current stakes in a kind of contest between two pioneering figures of this new science that was still very much in search of a way forward.

Jung, from the outset, expressed reservations with regard to Freud's insistence on the preponderant role of sexuality while acknowledging the fundamental discovery constituted by his emphasis on the existence of the unconscious and its role as indicated by, among other things, the observation of hysterical manifestations. Jung was to state later on that the incredibly bold nature of these early hypotheses on the operations of the unconscious psyche had been far from fully appreciated.

Freud expressed dismay at, as well as interest in, Jung's assertions concerning his ability to treat psychosis successfully. This had been the subject of Jung's doctoral dissertation, "The Psychology of Dementia Praecox," which he had sent to Freud on its publication in 1906. Freud recognized that, in this field, Jung possessed experience, a spirit of boldness, and a quality of intuition that he himself lacked.

It was in March 1907 (and not at the end of February, as stated by Ernest Jones) that the two men actually met for the first time in Freud's home in Vienna. Emma, according to a letter written by Carl in advance of the meeting, had "relieved him of all obligations" for the period of the stay in Vienna (McGuire 1974, 16J). She accompanied him to Vienna, the third member of the party being Carl's friend and colleague Ludwig Binswanger. The visit lasted only a few days; afterward Jung took his wife to Budapest and, from there, for a holiday in Italy.

After the customary greetings and courtesy exchanges, the two protagonists of the theory and practice of psychoanalysis engaged in a historic tête-à-tête. The dialogue between Freud and Jung was, from the beginning, both deep and extremely open. Their first discussion kept them awake late into the night. This meeting had been prepared at great length, and each of them came to it with his own convictions, doubts, and reservations. Yet both were imbued with the same passion, namely, a deep and essential concern for the soul within the human psyche, a concern based on their utter certainty that an understanding of this psyche was of absolutely vital significance for the health of the human being.

This decisive first meeting with Freud was a powerfully emotional experience for Carl, filling him with deep admiration for this truly remarkable and impressive man. He later shared his first impressions with Emma, expressing his sense of wonder at the impact of the encounter and the promise it held out for the future. The two men's respective discoveries, which they now so excitedly began to share, had lifted the veil behind which the reality of the human psyche had been concealed, causing an invigorating and radically fresh wind to blow through and beyond their professional milieu. Such novelty inevitably triggered sometimes violent opposition from fellow psychiatrists, and the two men were, for this reason, in need of one another's reassurance, Freud especially, for he, unlike Jung, had begun to suffer from the weight of advancing age. In a touching burst of self-revelation, Freud wrote to Jung after this first meeting: "I am sure you will not abandon the work, you have gone into it too deeply and seen for yourself how exciting, how far-reaching and how beautiful our subject is" (McGuire 1974, 18F).

The feelings of strong friendship allied with deep mutual admiration that were sparked between the two men are in all likelihood unequalled in the history of psychoanalysis and depth psychology. Two tremendous personalities revealed their true selves and discovered one another with a passionate enthusiasm and excitement.

While each of the two had some reservations concerning certain of the other's theoretical positions and conclusions, Jung valued Freud's criticism, for it was, he conceded, the fruit of "justified" opposition (McGuire 1974, 9J). The two men stepped up their correspondence and took advantage of subsequent opportunities for further meetings at various congresses and on the occasion of a sea voyage to the United States in 1909. It was not long before Freud and Jung came to be regarded as together representing the vanguard of the still youthful psychoanalytic movement, which was encountering an enthusiastic following in Europe and the United States.

Emma Jung, meanwhile, quite spontaneously carved out for herself a choice position in the relationship between these two men. This was an achievement that she owed to her personal ability, her intelligence, her knowledge, and her understanding. Emma's action was alternately that of an enlightened ambassador and that of a mediator. In her calm and determined presence, the age factor may be said to have dwindled into insignificance, and yet it should not be forgotten that Emma was only twenty-six years old and that Freud was twice her age.

The relationship was further enriched by the sincere and affectionate friendship that immediately developed between the two couples and the two families. At their first meeting, while the two husbands were locked in conversation together, Emma was the guest of Freud's wife, Martha. The two women took to one another from the start and immediately became friends. Both wives had the responsibility of large families. Their husbands were devoted to the same work heart and soul, and as pioneers and physicians of the psyche, they drew admiration and respect but also controversy. The encounter of these two men with one another had relieved each of them of a sense of solitude; it was a meeting in which their wives also participated and by which both women's lives were enriched.

The differences of age, background, and character were manifest, as both Freud and Jung were well aware. Such differences could prove complementary; in some cases, they held a certain charm and could actually represent an asset that reinforced the relationship.

Martha Freud, a Jewess, was deeply religious, but her convictions were those of a religion from which her husband had chosen to take his distance. Emma, under Carl's influence, had also distanced herself from her family's membership in the Reformed Church and from any regular religious practice.

Martha Freud devoted her time and energy principally to her family occupations and to playing the role of a genuinely kind hostess. Her family life was regulated in accordance with Professor Freud's strict professional schedule. Emma, meanwhile, was more closely involved in her husband's professional life, enjoyed greater freedom, and was quite determined not to neglect the life and development of her mind. Without laying claim to any special merit, Emma had, since marrying Carl, shared in her husband's research activity, typed reports on his findings, and cooperated in the writing of his first books. As far as Carl was concerned, his wife was someone with whom he felt perfectly free and able to share and discuss all these professional matters.

Mathilde, the Freuds' eldest daughter, was already of marriageable age. Emma took pleasure in allowing this young woman to take her around Vienna. Carl too showed his affection for the Freuds as a family. Emma and Carl's family life was at an earlier stage; their family was still growing. When Franz, their first and only son, was born in 1908 Carl announced the birth to Freud in an emotionally charged letter:

> You can imagine our joy. The birth went off normally, mother and child are doing well. Too bad we aren't peasants any more. Otherwise I could say: Now that I have a son I can depart in peace. A great deal more could be said on this complex theme. (McGuire 1974, 117J)

Freud was highly appreciative of Emma's qualities. He was impressed by her intellectual caliber and by her active involvement in her husband's professional life. He liked to give her flowers, made a point of praising her naturally charming manners, and would ask for her opinion in order to show how much he valued her judgment. For a short period he was even her analyst, an experience that undoubtedly further strengthened the positive feeling between them. Whenever any kind of conflict or disagreement was in the air, it was frequently Emma who wrote to Freud, who at one point commented that she was well known to him as a "solver of riddles" (McGuire 1974, 270F). Freud was not shy about expressing his admiration for Emma. He wrote to Carl: "Give your charming, clever and ambitious wife the pleasure of saving you from losing yourself in the business of money" (McGuire 1974, 266F).

In her capacity as Jung's coworker, Emma was even called upon to deal personally with the organization of the Nuremberg Congress in March 1910, since Carl had been called away suddenly to see a client in Chicago. At this time she wrote to Freud, reassuring him that everything was under control, while modestly downplaying her own role in ensuring that this was the case:

> Many thanks for your kind letter and offer of help which
> I shall gladly accept if anything more difficult happens.
> I can set your mind at rest by telling you that a young
> friend and pupil of my husband's, Dr Honneger, is depu-
> tizing with the patients and looking after the Nuremberg
> business with me, otherwise I would be rather nervous
> about everything turning out all right. (McGuire 1974,
> EJ March 16, 1910)

It is actually something of a miracle that we still have these few letters written by Emma to Freud, that they should have been preserved. Freud had kept them separately from Jung's letters to him, and when Freud died in 1939, it is probable that Emma found no way of asking that they be returned to her, as she subsequently did with letters addressed to other correspondents. Six letters written by Emma to Freud have thus survived. Three specific situations prompted her to communicate by this means with the "Dear Professor," in some cases without her husband's knowledge. The most dramatic of these situations was the Sabina affair. A more prosaic situation, namely the organization of the Weimar congress in 1911, was the subject of two of the letters. At a later date Emma was so bold as to give expression to her concern about the evolution of the relationship between Freud and her husband and to question Freud about this delicate matter.

Let us now backtrack somewhat and turn our attention to the Sabina affair, viewing it as a kind of Chinese shadow play that developed during the years 1904 to 1908. While the most affected parties were Emma and Jung, Freud also became involved in the plot, the central character of which was the young woman Sabina Spielrein. Sabina had become Jung's patient in 1904 on her arrival in Zürich from Russia, accompanied by her mother, for she was at the time only nineteen years old. The girl had been suffering from acute symptoms of mental breakdown, and her new physician, the young psychiatrist Carl Gustav Jung, who was at this time still in the early stages of coming to grips with the complexities of psychoanalytical theory and practice, threw himself into the business of treating the young woman, whom he saw every day without asking any fee for his services. Jung was fascinated and impressed by young Sabina's remarkable personality. Two years after her arrival, the psychotic episodes were a thing of the past, and Sabina, with Jung's encouragement, was able to begin her medical studies in Zürich.

Little by little the therapeutic relationship had turned into a friendship and ultimately into a love affair. The initiative in this direction had been taken by Sabina; at least, such was Jung's feeling on the matter. He seems not to have consciously seen this development coming, and he subsequently stated that he had fallen prey to a combination of blindness and naïveté, somewhat like Odysseus to whom Hermes issues the following warning in book 10 of the *Odyssey*: "Luckless man, why are you walking thus alone over these hills, in country you do not know?" (Homer 1980, 120).

Over a period of four years, Jung tried to gain control of the situation, but the spark had turned into a blaze that continued to spread. Emma, the young wife, still living at the Burghölzli at the time, had been unable to overcome her jealousy and the uncertainty that the shocking situation had caused to hover over the future of her marriage. By means of an anonymous letter—which Sabina claimed was written by Jung's wife—it seems that Emma, in a state of despair, had contacted the girl's parents, who were in this way informed of the situation that had developed between the analyst and his patient (Carotenuto 1977). The purpose of the letter, no doubt, had been to provoke Carl into reacting and to prompt some clarification of the situation on the part of the young Sabina. In Zürich rumors were rife, as can well be imagined.

Sabina's parents, feeling called upon to intervene, rushed to Zürich from their home in Moscow. In a letter to Freud in 1909, Sabina recounted her father's reaction in relation to Jung:

> My father said [referring to Jung] that they looked upon
> him like a god but he is, after all, only a man like any
> other. [He said] I'm delighted that she slapped him. I
> would have done exactly the same in her place. Let her do
> whatever she thinks necessary. She's old enough to deal
> with the situation. (Carotenuto 1977)

Jung's account of what happened was that he had done his utmost to help a gifted and intelligent girl, whose tremendous potential he had rapidly become aware of, but that he had allowed himself to be carried away on account of his excessive naïveté. Without a set of practical guidelines, in the absence of the protective boundary provided by deontology, fascination had gained the upper hand. As for Sabina, young and in the grip of her passion, she had been oblivious to any moral argument, had wanted to have a child by Jung, and had urged him to leave his wife. Jung had ended up admitting that he was indeed attracted to her.

It seems reasonable to suppose that Sabina was, as we would say nowadays, caught up in an erotic father transference in her relationship with Jung. It also seems very likely that she became the bearer of what Jung would later call an anima projection, that is, a projection of his feminine unconscious side. Pinned down in the depths of unconscious forces to which he had become prey, Jung no longer had the means of gaining any distance from the situation.[7] Perhaps he deliberately refused to analyze the signs of this attraction. It is undoubtedly of paramount importance that the analyst decode the emotions that are prompted by every analytical relationship. Are we to assume that Jung was, at this point, still ignorant of the realities of the countertransference, which is the translation or betrayal of the analyst's projections onto his or her patient?

It may have been the case that Carl and Emma had already begun to allow the intensity of their marital relationship to wane. Emma, quite naturally, was very much taken up with caring for her children, who arrived in rather quick succession, and there was considerable pressure on the couple from a combination of social, family, and professional sources. Yet, triggered by this incident, a deep and complex reality was forced upward toward the light of day: one of the strong and important components of Carl Gustav Jung's personality thereby stood revealed.

At the very beginning of the relationship with Sabina, in 1904, Carl was twenty-nine, Emma twenty-two, and Sabina nineteen or twenty. Four years passed. Carl, who had never sought to conceal his taste for women, at this point apparently discovered his polygamous instinct. Emma must have experienced incredulity and dismay along with deep hurt at this excruciatingly painful blow to her love for and fidelity toward her husband. Human drama along these lines is, of course, utterly commonplace. At the same time, this particular case

7. At the time of these events, the anima archetype had not yet been elaborated by Jung. Having learned a lesson from this painful experience and others that were to follow, he later devised this concept and developed its numerous symbolic aspects. The reader who wishes to know more at this stage may consult the commentary contained in Emma Jung's paper "Animus and Anima" (see chapter 11, where we deal with Emma's writings).

grew to become an immensely complex matter as its ramifications spread from the private world of the parties concerned finally to affect a whole family, a community, a city. The scandal even reached Vienna, for Freud himself was summoned to take sides in this fraught romantic episode. Freud was thus placed in the position of witnessing his friends' marital conflict. Carl, Emma, and Sabina all went to him for help, and he could hardly refuse to provide a listening ear. Moreover, he was expected to arbitrate the rights and wrongs of the affair, to calm the troubled waters, to offer good advice. This dramatic imbroglio engendered a collision between differing levels of reality and enabled Freud to become aware of Jung's weaknesses, among other things, as Carl revealed to him an aspect of his intimate self. In a letter that was both modest and deeply sincere, Jung took Freud into his confidence:

> A complex is playing Old Harry with me: a woman
> patient, whom years ago I pulled out of a sticky neurosis
> with greatest devotion, has violated my confidence and
> my friendship in the most mortifying way imaginable.
> She has kicked up a vile scandal solely because I denied
> myself the pleasure of giving her a child. I have always
> acted the gentleman towards her, but before the bar of
> my rather too sensitive conscience I nevertheless don't
> feel clean, and that is what hurts the most because my
> intentions were always honourable. . . . Meanwhile I
> have learnt an unspeakable amount of marital wisdom,
> for until now I had a totally inadequate idea of my
> polygamous components. Now I know where and how
> the devil can be laid by the heels. These painful yet
> extremely salutary insights have churned me up hellishly
> inside but for that very reason, I hope, have secured me
> moral qualities which will be to the greatest advantage to
> me in later life. The relationship with my wife has gained
> enormously in assurance and depth. (McGuire 1974, 133J)

Much earlier in the correspondence, Jung had referred to his "rich marriage," confessing to Freud that it had brought him great happiness, even though he had been turned down when he first proposed (McGuire 1974, 9J). This marriage, whether consciously or otherwise, had satisfied Jung's need for social recognition. His chosen bride was possessed of remarkable qualities and had received a highly principled upbringing. Thanks to his wife's family fortune, Carl was free of all financial worry. While Emma was undoubtedly introverted in nature, there could be no doubt that she was in love. Carl had written, at this earlier point in his marriage, that he both loved and respected Emma: "I am happy with my wife in every way" (McGuire 1974, 9J).

On a much later occasion, whether in a spirit of flippancy or realism, Jung stated that "the prerequisite for a good marriage, it seems to me, is the licence to be unfaithful" (McGuire 1974, 175J). Polygamy, he added, represented the wisdom of the Muslim religion, and in France it was considered quite normal for men to have mistresses as well as wives. And yet he was unhappy. He needed Emma and was aware of her suffering. In the same burst of confession and self-revelation, he acknowledged that he could not suppress his attraction to women. In the deepest sense, he was fascinated by them. "His libido is strong and possessive," wrote one of Jung's very close friends, Godwin Baynes (Baynes Jansen 2003, 211).

It is absolutely no secret that Jung was possessed of strong sex appeal. Women succumbed to his attraction. Was this a narcissistic need on his part for recognition? He admitted his own doubts on this score. If it were a question of his anima, how was he to become conscious of a phenomenon that experience alone would teach him to recognize and to which he would finally give a name, but only after considerable hesitation?

Given the complexity of the situation, what else could Freud do but listen and wonder in the privacy of his own mind about its many deeply subtle and possibly unspoken aspects? Quite possibly as a way of sympathizing, Freud admitted that his own marriage had known better times and that his pleasures nowadays were confined to contemplating the youthfulness and future of his children. This, at any rate, is what he told Emma, who was rather disconcerted by the information, as she confessed in her letter to Freud on November 6, 1911. By speaking to the young woman of his own experience in this way, Freud no doubt believed that he was sharing the concern that was causing her such pain and worry. But Carl and Emma's situation was quite different: not only were they still young, but their respective personalities meant that their demands and expectations were radically different.

Emma was at this time a young woman in a state of shock, badly hurt, upset, and deeply wounded. Freud, who was of a similar age to the father she had recently lost, sought to offer her affection and understanding. She did not know where her marriage was heading and felt ill-used by a husband whose vitality and creativity were such that they caused her to feel overwhelmed and, on occasion, crushed. In a state of bewilderment and feeling unsure of herself, Emma touchingly looked to Freud for reassurance, confiding in him, without directly naming Sabina, the serious problem represented for her by the discovery of Carl's character and inclinations:

> Usually I am quite at one with my fate and see very well how lucky I am, but from time to time I am tormented by the conflict about how I can hold my own against Carl. I find I have no friends, all the people who associate with us really only want to see Carl . . . . Naturally the women are all in love with him, and with the men I am instantly cordoned off as the wife of the father or friend. . . . Carl too says that I should stop concentrating on him and the children, but what on earth am I to do? (McGuire 1974, EJ November 24, 1911)

How could the reader of this letter not feel affection and respect for the sincerity and humility displayed by Emma, whose soul was so painfully flayed by the whiplash of this first crisis? While Emma's self-esteem was so deeply undermined, Sabina gave no thought whatsoever to the moral consequences of her behavior. She made light of Emma's feelings carelessly, was perhaps even quite oblivious of them. While not so very many years older than Sabina, Emma was a wife and mother, imbued with a keen sense of her responsibilities and commitments. From her heart a legitimate anger, weighted with a terrible anguish, was liable to spring forth. Carl was caught up in an ambivalent position heavily draped with shadow. This was just the beginning of Emma's inner questioning of her husband in a confrontation that was to inhabit her soul and cause her torment for so much of her life.

With the passage of time, the emotional storm triggered by Sabina Spielrein calmed down. Sabina left Zürich for Vienna. The tempestuous outbursts were quelled, and the painful sting inflicted by passion became less acute. It is no doubt important to record here that Sabina made a significant contribution to furthering psychoanalytical theory along simultaneously Jungian and Freudian lines. She had Jung to thank for his skill in enabling her to overcome, in a relatively short time, the serious hysterical disorder that had been attributable, at least to some extent, to the damaging relationship she had witnessed between her parents. Jung, perceiving her talents, had encouraged her to develop her intuitions and her remarkable intellectual qualities.

What Sabina owed Freud was her acceptance within his circle of initiates in Vienna, where she was one of the very few women to be admitted. The new science of psychoanalysis benefited from two important contributions by Sabina Spielrein: her doctoral thesis, entitled "The Psychological Content of a Case of Schizophrenia," and, above all, a paper entitled "Destruction as the Cause of Coming into Being." As happened on other occasions, Jung took inspiration from his patient's work in his own writing.

And an additional factor to Sabina's credit is that she herself became a brilliant psychoanalyst.[8]

Freud and Jung had laid the foundations of a solid international organization. Emma had given birth to her and Carl's fourth child, a daughter, Marianne. Carl had resigned from his position at the Burghölzli hospital, and the Jung family was finally able to settle in a new home in the countryside. And so we come to the period 1909–1910.

Jung sent Freud a copy of his new book *Symbols of Transformation*, in which he set out a view very different from that of Freud on the origin and the scope of libido, which Jung regarded as, above all, a fundamental energy of the psyche. Jung was well aware that this act of intellectual dissidence, this theoretical divergence, might cause upset to Freud. Was this publication then to be regarded as a virtually deliberate act of disloyalty on the part of Freud's heir? Emma knew the work in detail, for she had been entrusted with the task of clarifying the etymology of the Latin words used in the text. While sharing Carl's views concerning the theoretical propositions put forward, she feared Freud's reaction and the possibility of rejection or opposition on his part.

In a conciliatory but courageous letter to Freud, Emma expressed support for her husband's position. Her wish was that the two of them should find a way of openly airing their divergent positions, for otherwise their differing opinions risked casting a shadow over their good relations:

> Since your visit I have been tormented by the idea that
> your relation with my husband is not altogether as it
> should be, and since it definitely ought not to be like

---

8. One of her patients in Geneva, where she lived for many years after her marriage, was Jean Piaget, the eminent child psychologist who gained an international reputation. She returned to Russia after the Revolution, toward the end of the 1920s, where her life ended tragically. She was murdered, together with her two daughters, by the Nazis in the synagogue at Rostov in 1942 at the age of fifty-one. The episodes and events briefly alluded to here indicate the highly complex nature of Sabina Spielrein's life and tragic destiny.

this I want to try to do whatever is in my power. I do not
know whether I am deceiving myself when I think you
are somehow not in agreement with *Symbols of Transformation*. . . . It would do you both so much good if you got
down to a thorough discussion of it. (McGuire 1974, EJ
October 3, 1911)

I knew how eagerly Carl was waiting for your opinion.
(McGuire 1974, EJ November 6, 1911)

Carl was no doubt ignorant of the fact that his wife had written
to Freud in an effort to get them to speak of their differences. Much
later, in his book *Memories, Dreams, Reflections*, he gave expression
to what had been his own fears at this time:

When I was working on my book about the libido and
approaching the end of the chapter "The Sacrifice," I
knew in advance that its publication would cost me my
friendship with Freud. . . . Freud . . . could not grasp the
spiritual significance of incest as a symbol. I knew that
he would never be able to accept any of my ideas on this
subject.
    I spoke to my wife about this, and told her of my fears.
She attempted to reassure me, for she thought that Freud
would magnanimously raise no objections, although he
might not accept my views. (Jung 1961, 167)

Freud, in actual fact, was ambivalent. He admired Jung's original
and progressive views which served the cause of science and represented the basis of their mutual esteem. If Freud had raised Jung to
the highest position in the hierarchy of the psychoanalytical broth-
erhood, it was because Jung was, up to that point, the only one of
his followers in whom he had complete trust. Jung's prestige and
powerful intellect were such that they would guarantee the future of

the psychoanalytical movement as it continued to grow in strength. Freud badly needed him. At the important Weimar congress in 1911 the vitality of psychoanalysis was proclaimed, and this gathering represented its consecration.

Freud was not, however, indifferent to Jung's increasing success. Emma, with her subtle perceptiveness, found a way of referring to this aspect in her letter of November 6, 1911. Was Freud afraid that his star might be growing dimmer while Jung's was rising and growing brighter? Emma, who was truly and deeply fond of Freud, suggested that a certain father/son complex had to be transcended in the interest of better cooperation. Alas, her affection and respect for Freud met with no echo. Emma was powerless to contain a nagging and insidiously expanding bitterness.

This state of disaffection was, lamentably, to transform the years of intense friendship into a virulent opposition that other supporters of Freud would find ways of fueling, thereby poisoning all warmth and good feeling between the two men. Ernest Jones championed Freud without ever gaining for himself the immense admiration that Freud had felt for Jung. Yet it was to Jones that Freud complained: "Jung seems beside himself, he's behaving in a completely crazy manner . . . our common interest is beginning to demand an official separation" (Paskauskas 1995, 186).

Could things have turned out differently? Or was the break that by now had become inevitable engraved in the destiny of these two pioneers? The tremendous respect and admiration that they had felt for one another had enabled the psychoanalytical movement to rise, spread, and achieve its full embodiment. Yet theoretical divergence seems not to have been the only cause of the separation. The two men's differing psychological structures, combined with their differing conceptions of the unconscious, was, in the view of some commentators, the twofold factor that gradually generated resentment and spite, extending, in the case of Freud, to the uttering of calumny. Jung, it seems, deeply desired the preservation of the relationship, while arguing for mutual respect for their complementary visions.

The consequences of this split for the future of the psychoanalytical movement were heavy. But the process that was to end in a painful and tragic severing of relations had by now been set in motion. Jung later offered an explanation of what had happened, expressed in terms of his own categories, in one of his important works, *Psychological Types*. Freud, after reading it, had the audacity to write to Jones that it was "the work of a snob and a mystic," which sounds painfully like the sour grapes of an old man who has been mercilessly sidelined (Paskauskas 1995, 423–424).

There had arisen, temporarily on the same pedestal, two figures of genius whose intuitions were profoundly complementary. Neither, in his inner world, would ever forget the other, even if all outer contact between the two men was ultimately to cease forever. Thanks to this exceptional relationship, the foundations of a radically new and revolutionary approach to the life of the psyche had been laid. It is possible that this separation was indeed necessary in order to supply this science with the tools of its development. Emma did not seek to conceal her true sadness and inability to understand how things could have come to such a pass. For her personally, the end of the partnership represented a painful blow. She thereby lost a source of support and an extremely good friend, but in her capacity as Jung's wife and coworker compromise was out of the question, and there was no other way forward.

Freud, toward the end of his life, admitted that the break with Jung had represented a great loss. Jung went even further, stating that, without the discovery by Freud of "Freudian psychoanalysis," he would have lacked the essential key required to lay the foundation of his own scientific convictions: "Freud became vitally important to me, especially because of his fundamental researches into the psychology of hysteria and of dreams" (Jung 1961, 114). "Like an Old Testament prophet, he undertook to overthrow false gods, to rip the veils away from a mass of dishonesties and hypocrisies, mercilessly expressing the rottenness of the contemporary psyche" (ibid., 169).

Although Jung did, indeed, experience moments of uncertainty, it is not difficult to imagine that, in the course of time, he would have come to feel too severely constrained by the confining role of heir or successor in which he had been placed by Freud. Contemporaries who were close to Jung testified to his painful dilemma, acknowledging that a man with such a powerful personality and overflowing creativity, permanently on the move in search of new ideas, represented a law unto himself. The only law to which Jung remained faithful, over and above all else, was indeed his creative drive and on behalf of this he would have been prepared to sacrifice anything or everything else.

The same kind of pressure from Jung's inner world influenced and, to some extent, dictated the terms of his relationships with women. His personal mandate for self-development drove him beyond all the frontiers laid down by others in the search to redefine the territorial boundaries of emotional involvement in accordance with the demands of his own psyche. The role of this powerful inner drive certainly did not soften the impact of whatever emotional difficulties and choices Jung encountered on his path. This overriding drive was then, in the final analysis, the force at work here, and it may be said, in this case, to have predestined the break with Freud. It was thus that Emma found herself inevitably exposed, without any cushioning of the blows, to these sharp and unexpected twists of fate imposed by the inner demands of her husband's intemperate nature. By this time, it was becoming very clear that she would have to work quite alone in the effort to define her own place, her own future, and her own priorities.

The last flames of the friendship between Freud and Jung blazed at the Weimar congress in 1911. Emma, who had helped organize the gathering, attended it as a matter of course in her capacity as Jung's coworker. Her husband, in a burst of what may be seen as a perverse form of candor, had had the audacity to propose to Freud that they also invite to the congress a young woman whose superior intelligence and subtle understanding of psychic phenomena he had had occasion to discover. The woman was Toni Wolff. Emma, out of generosity and magnanimity, expressed her delight that Carl should have encountered among his patients such a gifted woman.

Carl, irresistibly attracted by Toni's fine mind and mysterious erotic power, was to ignore Circe's likewise firm recommendation to Odysseus:

> You will come to the Sirens first of all; they bewitch any
> mortal who approaches them . . . . Give your crew orders
> to bind you both hand and foot as you stand upright
> against the mast-stay, with the rope-ends tied to the mast
> itself; thus you may hear the two Sirens' voices and be
> enraptured. If you implore your crew and beg them to re-
> lease you, then they must bind you fast with more bonds
> again. (Homer 1980, 143)

Once again, regarding his fascination as something unavoidable, Jung allowed his marriage vows to slip out of the picture. In justification of his behavior and attitude, he claimed that it met with his wife's tacit approval. The arrival of Toni Wolff in Carl and Emma's professional, family, and married life was to leave deep and indelible traces from this point onward.

This young woman's presence at the 1911 congress proved to be important for Emma, as we will see in the next chapter. Toni Wolff was propelled to the very heart of Emma Jung's life at the same time that she became a central figure for her husband Carl. One of the Jung descendants expressed regret that this woman—a thorn in Emma's side, the cause of such intolerable suffering—should be accorded a place in a text focusing on Emma's life. But to ignore her presence would be quite unforgivable. And we may also ask to what extent Toni was actually to blame. Why did Jung, at a time when a break with Sigmund Freud was imminent, propose, to all appearances quite innocuously, that the young woman Toni Wolff should attend the Weimar congress? In doing so, perhaps innocently or unconsciously, yet seemingly quite frivolously, Jung let the wolf into the sheep pen.

Who can take it upon themselves to judge such acts? This is the mystery spoken of and represented in myths and Greek tragedies. Man is the prey of his passions, his blindness, his need to push back the frontiers of his ignorance, to enact the visions of his soul. And the gods appear to derive such pleasure and satisfaction from these spectacles.

Already deprived of a highly valued friendship by the dramatic cessation of the relationship between Freud and Jung, Emma was once again obliged to adjust her position as wife in order to accommodate the polygamous aspects of her husband's personality. Her predicament inevitably brings to mind the sad and lonely fate bemoaned by Penelope:

> As for myself, the god has assigned me a grief that has
> no bounds. My life is one of melancholy and mourning,
> though during daytime I take some pleasure in looking
> to my own tasks in the house, and my women's tasks; but
> when night comes and everyone else is lost in sleep, I lie
> in my bed while poignant cares come thronging about my
> restless heart. (Homer 1980, 240)

FIGURE I.

Emma Rauschenbach as a young bride, 1903.
© *Jung Family Archives.*

FIGURE 2.

The Jung family at the Château d'Œx, 1917.
© *Jung Family Archives.*

FIGURE 3.

Emma Jung at Eranos, 1938.
© *Jung Family Archives.*

FIGURE 4.
Emma and Carl Gustav Jung at Bollingen, 1953.
© *Jung Family Archives.*

FIGURE 5.

The Rauschenbach home, Ölberg, at Schaffhausen,
where Emma spent her adolescence.

Credit: Imelda Gaudissart.

FIGURE 6.

The Burghölzli.

Credit: Imelda Gaudissart.

FIGURE 7.

The entryway at the Jungs' home in Küsnacht.

Credit: Imelda Gaudissart.

FIGURE 8.

The boathouse at Küsnacht.

Credit: Imelda Gaudissart.

FIGURE 9.

The only remaining example of Jung's pebble constructions.

Credit: Imelda Gaudissart.

FIGURE 10.

The tower at Bollingen.

Credit: Alain Desarzens.

FIGURE 11.

The Psychology Club of Zurich.

Credit: Imelda Gaudissart.

FIGURE 12.

Stele engraved by Carl Gustav Jung
in memory of Emma, Bollingen, 1956.

Credit: Imelda Gaudissart.

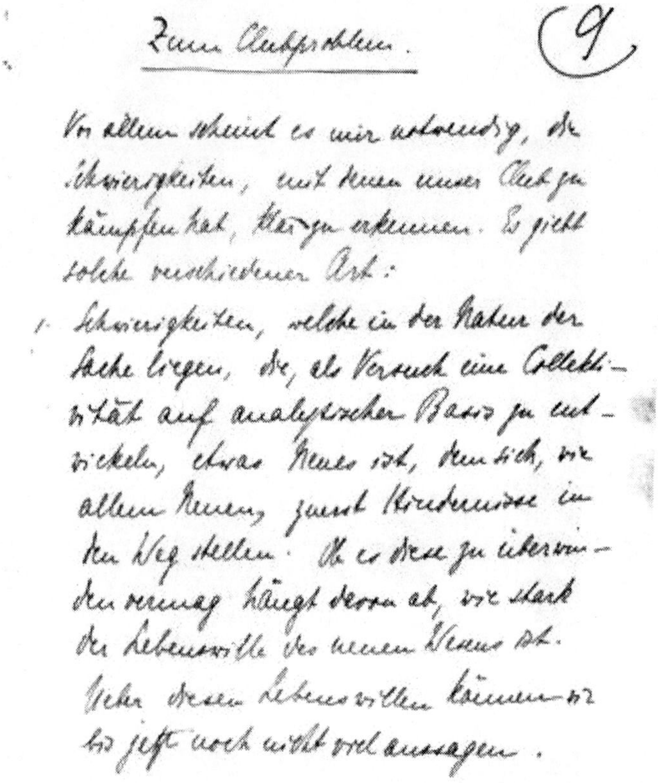

Zum Clubproblem.   (9)

Vor allem scheint es mir notwendig, die
Schwierigkeiten, mit denen unser Club zu
kämpfen hat, klar zu erkennen. Es giebt
solche verschiedener Art:

1. Schwierigkeiten, welche in der Natur der
Sache liegen, die, als Versuch eine Collekti-
vität auf analytischer Basis zu ent-
wickeln, etwas Neues ist, dem sich, wie
allem Neuen, zuerst Hindernisse in
den Weg stellen. Ob es diese zu überwin-
den vermag hängt davon ab, wie stark
der Lebenswille des neuen Vereins ist.
Über diesen Lebenswillen können wir
bis jetzt noch nicht viel aussagen.

FIGURE 13.

Emma Jung's handwriting.

$$5$$

$$\blacksquare$$

Family Life at Küsnacht:
Emma, Carl, and Toni Wolff

This chapter focuses on the nature and development of the marriage relationship between Emma and Carl Gustav Jung and on aspects of the highly complex situation engendered by it. While to all outward appearances Emma and Carl formed a rather typical married couple of the early twentieth century, the disturbed inner depths of their relationship generated some unexpected outcomes that were attributable in largely equal measure to Carl Gustav Jung's extraordinary personality and to the manner in which Emma responded to her husband's unusual way of being and, particularly, his untoward attitude to his marriage. While their roles in this partnership were for neither of them the result of a deliberate choice, the behavior of each over time and in the course of their respective and shared commitments endows their story with a truly unusual significance and value.

To provide a full description of forty years of family life at Küsnacht would be an impossible task. We will have to be content to present just a few select episodes, a handful of representative or specific scenes, and in that way hope to meet the challenge of offering some of the flavor of the prevailing atmosphere and some of the predominant hues of a much broader canvas, rather as if we were attempting an inevitably imperfect reconstitution of an ancient mosaic from its scant surviving sections. As in a Chinese shadow play, we will be aware, above all, of outlines and movements, so that it will be up to the imagination to fill in the gaps.

The move to the new house at Küsnacht was a relief for all concerned. Life at the Burghölzli had become difficult, cramped, and complicated. Apart from the professional tensions and the lack of space for a growing family, an important consideration was Jung's personal desire for the freedom to organize and conduct his work in his own preferred manner. Emma's overriding need was to have a house that would be suitable for family life as she conceived of it. Both Carl and Emma accordingly wished to make their home in a spacious residence that would enable them to benefit from a protective haven while offering a convivial setting for both family and professional activities.

This does not mean, of course, that the move to Küsnacht was easy or straightforward. A large number of people were involved. Jung actually complained in a letter to Freud that it was all too much for him, that it had been an exceptionally miserable week, and that he had been "quite unable to concentrate on a thing." "Only my wife," he added, "has kept her head above water" (McGuire 1974, 142J). Such a comment at least represented a fine compliment to Emma, who had evidently succeeded in managing the difficulties and coping with the demands of the move much better than her husband. Her excellent sense of organization, her discreetly efficient behavior and ability to prioritize, had enabled her to deal with the myriad aspects of this demanding situation.

In any effort to describe the Jungs' new life in Küsnacht, a search for the truth once again brings to light subtle layers of contrast and complexity. The words that Carl had engraved in Latin above the majestic front door of their new home supply more than a hint of the deep satisfaction and intense joy experienced by the couple at this stage in their lives:

Anno MCMVIII
Carolus Gustavus Jung
Emma Rauschenbach
Uxor eius hanc
Villam ridenti
In loco otioso
Erig.Iuss.[9]

Just as the Ölberg property remained in the Homberger-Rauschenbach family through successive generations, so the Küsnacht house has, for more than a century now, been lived in by Emma and Carl Jung's children and grandchildren. During the years after Emma's death, Carl Gustav went on living there until his own death in 1961.[10]

It was during the year following the move from the Burghölzli to Küsnacht that Emma gave birth to their fourth child, Marianne. These years—1909 and 1910—coincided with the highest point and beginning of the decline of the relationship between Freud and Jung, as well as with the repercussions and troubling outcome of the Sabina affair.

Emma and Carl had arranged for Carl's mother, Emilie, and his younger sister, Trudi, to move into a house not far from their own new home. This was an arrangement that suited everyone. Thanks to this move, Emilie Jung was able to enjoy more comfortable living conditions, while Trudi, who had remained unmarried, acted for a

---

9. An approximate translation might be, "In 1908 Carl Gustav Jung and his wife, Emma Rauschenbach, built this house in a cheerful, tranquil place."

10. After the parents, their only son, Franz, the architect, and his family moved into the house. Today one of Franz's sons, also an architect, continues to live there. The family very occasionally open the house and grounds to visitors keen to see the images and to experience the emotions associated with the location and residence that witnessed the elaboration of so many foundational concepts, the day-to-day life of the family, and Carl and Emma's professional lives. A book entitled *The House of C. G. Jung: The History and Restoration of the Residence of Emma and Carl Gustav Jung-Rauschenbach* by Andreas Jung, Regula Michel, and Judith Rohrer was published in 2010 by FO Print and Media AG, Abt Finanzen, telling the story of this house and of the persons who lived in it.

short period as secretary to her brother when Emma's duties no longer allowed her to perform this role.

When Emma and Carl were away from home, Emilie would come to stay with the children, who delighted in their grandmother's presence. She had a fertile imagination and a store of wild and fantastic tales to tell. Carl, in his own childhood and youth, had been marked by his mother's strange habits and imagination, and he undoubtedly would have said that these wild stories were generated by what he termed his mother's number 2 personality.

As the wife of the Protestant clergyman Paul Jung, Emilie had been completely immersed in a religious climate, and much earlier in her life she had experienced incidents that could be termed mediumistic. It was Emilie who, to some extent, took upon herself the role of familiarizing the children with bible stories and religious knowledge. Carl and Emma did not themselves regard religious education as an essential part of their children's upbringing. What was of paramount importance as far as they were concerned was that their children should develop the requisite psychological balance to enable them, when the time came, to make their own choices about how they wished to live their lives. The essential qualities that they as parents sought to inculcate into their children were thus an open mind, respect for others, and a coherent set of fundamental attitudes.

Emma's daily life continued charting its path between two poles that were quite distinct from one another in one sense and yet hardly far apart in practice. On the one hand, she had responsibility for her family; on the other, she had a deep personal need to develop her own thinking faculty, and this led her, in the course of time, to take up practice as a psychoanalyst. Her tasks as mother of a large family initially took up a great amount of her time, for although she had a good deal of domestic help with the chores, she herself kept a close eye on the many and varied needs of her large household. It was she who paid close attention to the children's schooling, and she also took charge of both managing the family budget and keeping the professional accounts.

Having been taught by her father about money matters at a young age, Emma was extremely capable when it came to accounting and the prudent management of financial resources. Carl was more than happy to leave this side of things to Emma because he was both over-worked and frequently away from home. As his fame and reputation grew, there was increasing pressure to be in more than one place at once. He wrote, for example, to Freud from Lugano on April 2, 1912: "At last I have got away from Zürich so as to be alone with myself for a few days before going to Florence with my wife . . . . I am on my own here and unknown and that is the acme of pleasure" (McGuire 1974, 310J).

This was a situation that initially required so much of the twenty-eight-year-old Emma's time that her intellectual pursuits had to be placed on the back burner, though her research on the Grail legend was never very far from her thoughts. Her choice of priority in this regard stemmed from her faithful commitment to her marriage vows, which she regarded in the light of a vocation. Even so, this freely chosen path in life did sometimes prompt in Emma doubts and questions about its sense and meaning. On September 10, 1912, in a burst of frank and open self-revelatory exchange with Freud, Emma wrote of the weight of her responsibilities and the toll that they represented on her time and energy:

> Carl was away nearly all summer; since Saturday he
> has been on the trip to America after spending only
> one day here between military service and departure.
> I have so much to do now that I can't let too much
> libido travel after him to America, it might so easily
> get lost on the way. (McGuire 1974, EJ September
> 9, 1912)

The list of Emma's responsibilities might seem endless. One of her priorities, alongside bringing up her children and overseeing their education, was to ensure that her husband enjoyed the requisite degree of comfort that would enable him to exercise his profession as analyst and conduct his research under optimal conditions. She received Carl's patients and also his students and disciples. At her husband's request, she actually began to assist him in the treatment of some of the patients. Under her hospitable roof, she received prominent figures who were passing through Zürich, as well as colleagues from the world of psychiatry and members of the family. The couple's social life outside the home was concentrated primarily in the circles generated by the world of professional psychology and psychoanalysis. Jung's reputation, which triggered adulation as well as virulent criticism, gave Emma cause for vigilance. While at pains to appear welcoming, she was at the same time concerned about preserving the family's private life from scrutiny by curious and sometimes malevolent onlookers.

Freud was, on more than one occasion, one of the Jungs' choice guests. In 1911 Jung had the opportunity to show him around his new home. The children took him out to see their lake, quite as if he were the grandfather they had never known. Emma was full of small attentions for this friend who had come to occupy such a very special place in her heart. Freud, for his part, had gone to the trouble of sending Emma some books in advance of his visit, the purpose of which was to prepare for the famous Weimar congress at which Jung was to act as president. Emma noticed that Carl was somewhat tense during Freud's visit. While she was already aware that her husband was indeed sometimes ill at ease in his friendships with men, the problem was exacerbated in this case by the first premonitory signs that were to lead to the definitive split between Freud and Jung. Emma, deeply sensitive to such manifestations, could not help feeling sadness and concern.

Where her own private relationship with her husband was concerned, Emma was not at this time feeling that there was cause for mistrust. It is to be remembered that Jung himself had been taken by surprise and thrown off course by the untoward development of his relation with Sabina. Evidence to this effect is supplied in a letter he wrote to Freud from Küsnacht. In an emotional moment and from the safe position of his trust in Freud, he had the momentary courage, or candor, to refer to these matters, claiming on the one hand that he was "the most innocent of spouses," while also confessing and acknowledging that he had made a very serious mistake for which he was truly sorry (McGuire 1974, 135J). This was at around the same time, not long after the move to Küsnacht, that Emma too wrote in confidence to Freud of her bewilderment in the wake of her husband's detour from the path of marital fidelity.

It is important also to repeat that the incident with Sabina Spielrein forced Emma to find ways of learning to put up with a tendency in her husband to which Carl now openly admitted. It was a state of affairs that was to affect Emma's life and emotions for several decades. Setting these events in the context of the Jungs' family life makes it possible to view them from another and particularly striking angle. Toni Wolff's subsequent appearance in C. G. Jung's life represented the factual baseline of what was to be a long, difficult to manage, uncomfortably complex, and painful relationship.

Carl at the time was thirty-five years old. Emma was twenty-eight, and Toni twenty-two. While Emma was not, in terms of years, so very much older than Toni, her circumstances had endowed her with considerable maturity and experience. Carl, as with Sabina previously, succumbed to the charm of Toni's brilliant mind. The young woman came to him initially as a patient and her quick cure was the result of Jung's formidable insight and ability. Toni, meanwhile, was totally in thrall to him. Their encounter was a meeting of minds which sparked a flame that was to burn fiercely for several decades.

There is surely no way that we could reasonably omit from this account a concise portrait of the woman who subsequently came to be referred to, in certain quarters, as "Jung's second wife." Toni Wolff was born in 1888 into one of the oldest and most respectable families of Zürich. She was the eldest of three sisters and enjoyed the status of heir to her father with whom she had a close and exclusive relationship, taking the place of a son. Having been brought up in an atmosphere of wealth, elegance, and culture, the three daughters were encouraged to acquire knowledge and to cultivate their minds.

At an early age, Toni began to show an interest in philosophy, mythology, and the history of religions. She already spoke French, and her father had sent her to England to learn English.[11] In spite of her love of study, Toni was unable to enroll as a student at the University of Zürich, for the Swiss universities were, at the time, sexist in the extreme. It was deemed quite inappropriate and unsuitable for the young ladies of the upper bourgeoisie to mix with the predominantly male student population. Toni had earlier formed a few short-lived romantic attachments, but she remained unmarried and continued to live in her parents' home up until her mother's death.

The death in 1909 of Arnold Wolff, at the age of sixty-three, was the event that precipitated his eldest daughter into Jung's life. Toni was so utterly bereft by this loss that she fell into a state of grave depression, initially rejecting the efforts of her mother, Anna, to help her deal with her distress. Nor did Toni's therapy with Jung yield any positive effects until the point at which, in a flash of brilliant intuition, he likened her depression to the events described in some of the Greek myths. This skillfully oriented amplification awakened Toni to her own reality. Thus was born the relationship that was to cast its dark shadow and subtle complexity over some thirty years of Emma and Carl's married life.

Emma, in this situation, found herself utterly disarmed. Her own love for her husband, her constant presence and concern for his welfare, seemed quite powerless to deflect the powerful rays of this attraction. Her position was thus one of terrible vulnerability as she experienced the pain of feeling cast aside, no longer party to her husband's primary concerns and interests. While it is certainly the case that Jung never deliberately intended to exclude his wife from his sentiments and concerns and continued to regard her as a privileged

---

11. Toni subsequently retained a deep love for and interest in all things British.

FAMILY LIFE AT KÜSNACHT

partner, it is equally true that his nature led him to turn his attention and feelings toward women who had more free time to devote
to him and whose admiration for their "master" was all-consuming.

It was in 1912 that the friendship between Freud and Jung broke
down once and for all. Although they subsequently exchanged the
occasional letter, the tone had become taut and functional, exclusively professional. Jung was upset in the extreme, as his own respect
for Freud remained unscathed. He continued to set an extremely
high value on this relationship, which had been truly exceptional
in its quality and was not without a significant component of dis-
placed paternal attachment.

As far as Freud was concerned, however, the views and ways of
thinking of the master were to be adhered to at all costs. There was
no room for a second master. This lack of recognition revived in
Jung the pain of having failed to establish a close relationship of
mutual respect with his own father.

Throughout this period of friction that heralded the complete
break between Jung and Freud, Emma sought to comfort Carl and
to tend his wounds, while taking his side and expressing her own
dismay at Freud's attitude. She encouraged her husband's pioneering work and shared his discoveries as well as his doubts and hesitations. She expressed support for Carl's intuitions, not out of love
alone but because she naturally and spontaneously shared his vision
of the springs of human behavior. Emma certainly had a mind of
her own, and it was with extreme lucidity that she observed the
passionate responses that were impelling the ruin of all that these
two committed men and thinkers had believed they could build
together. The end of the relationship inflicted a wound that would
never, during all the years remaining to them, become fully healed.
It unveiled, at the same time, a new horizon that was to open up the
way to dramatic events and promising developments.

The year 1913 saw the beginning of what was to be a radical, decisive, and unprecedented test of Jung's endurance and was con-
sequently to represent a grueling trial of Emma's own strength.

Was the onset of this experience generated by the break with Freud? Did it represent an essentially unavoidable ontological—or existential—necessity for Jung? Was it the consequence of the opening of the door to the collective unconscious which Jung had knowingly and deliberately unsealed by his close observation of the processes at work in the psychoses he sought to understand? A path such as this is not one on which any human being embarks voluntarily, for in all such cases it is the unconscious that has taken charge. What was imminent at this point was that Jung was about to plunge deep into the abysses of the life of the unconscious psyche and to experience this realm of terror unguided and unprotected by any form of safety net.

He was to be cast violently into unknown territories by real presences that sometimes showed their terrifying aspect and at other times their fantastic or fabulous faces. The territories into which Jung was venturing were uncharted. Where was he heading? What would be the outcome? We may, of course, remember Jonas and his enforced sojourn in the belly of the whale. Images from Dante's *Inferno* also come to mind. During this period, ancient tales and myths became Jung's immediate and frequently nightmarish experience in the companionship of which he gained firsthand knowledge of the symbolic representations of death and rebirth as they confronted one another.[12]

Jung was thirty-eight, about to enter the second half of his life, when he first began to move in this new and frightening direction. The descent into this radical inner experience was to provide the foundation for the gradual elaboration of the original path that his vision of the human psyche enabled him to chart, the path that would lead him to define the specific features of depth psychology. This experience inspired numerous books, including *The Psychology of the Transference* and *Psychology and Alchemy*, as well as many

---

12. In *The Red Book*, published in 2009, the reader can come closer to Jung's experiences during this period of confrontation with the unconscious.

others. In chapter 6 of *Memories, Dreams, Reflections*, entitled "Confrontation with the Unconscious," Jung set out to provide his own description and explanation of this transformative experience.

On a day-to-day basis, in relation to Jung's inner life and experiences, everything was totally unpredictable, and this created an atmosphere of uncertainty for all those around him. In order to preserve appearances and so as to maintain some form of salutary contact with the life of consciousness and normal everyday routine, Jung continued to see patients in the afternoon. His mornings were spent by the lake, sometimes in the company of his older children, where in all humility and with childlike pleasure he constructed a village out of pebbles. In the face of this utterly singular and equally unpredictable experience, Emma had to hold on and keep going, offering protection, working to maintain the order and outer harmony that might serve as solid tokens required to prevent the world from collapsing. It is undoubtedly not too bold a surmise to imagine that Carl, without Emma's unconditional presence and support, might well have lost his balance and broken down completely.

It was not without good reason, therefore, that Jung, many years later, wrote in *Memories, Dreams, Reflections* that he owed gratitude to his wife for her practical and moral support during this difficult time. For the time being, however, he was doing all but make life easy for his wife. While she was the rule to which he looked for support, the anchor to which he clung, it was Toni to whom he revealed, and with whom he discussed, the content that was emerging from his encounter with the unconscious. Was his wish to protect Emma? Was he afraid that he would drag her down into his inner tempest? Toni had already experienced the terrible suffering of a psychotic episode from which Jung had rescued her. In this capacity, as fellow sufferer, she was in a position to understand and share Jung's anguish. Yet, for Emma, such sharing on the part of another woman was experienced as an outrage, a source of incomprehensible pain and suffering.

We may suppose that Emma probably spoke about what she was forced to endure at this time with her mother, to whom she remained close. What advice could a mother, who had quite definitely encouraged her daughter's marriage to this particular man, offer her at this point? Bertha could not have been ignorant of the dominant personality traits that made her son-in-law such an eccentric and powerfully idiosyncratic individual. She had herself benefited from analytical treatment with him after the death of her own husband. Undoubtedly she felt gratitude toward him, as well as great admiration for his skills and reputation. Might she have been inclined, therefore, to turn a blind eye to the manifestations of his shadow?

Bertha, in all likelihood, would have encouraged her daughter to be more self-assertive. Carl himself declared more than once that living together was difficult. According to Deirdre Bair, Ludwig Binswanger stated that he had dreamed of Emma coming to him with complaints about her tyrannical husband, and Sabina Spielrein recounted a similar dream. Did Emma at any moment consider separation from her unfaithful husband? Her mind probably dwelled at times upon possibly similar marital scandals that had troubled and undermined the traditional and highly principled moral ground favored by the Swiss bourgeoisie of the period. Are we to imagine that Emma might have contemplated taking such a step?

The situation of her marriage was, to say the least, fragile, uncomfortable, and at times frankly unbearable. And yet Emma's steadfastness and upbringing prevented her from setting aside the responsibilities of marriage and family, which she continued to regard as a vocation. Over and above such considerations, her love for Carl and admiration for his uncontested genius remained unscathed. Never would she abandon the commitments by which she was bound, even if, during some of the darkest hours of pain and bewilderment, the fantasy of separation may indeed have crossed her mind.

In the midst of these torturous difficulties, Ölberg remained for Emma a refuge synonymous with a return to the happy setting and memories of her own childhood. Feast days and parties, holidays and periods when Carl was away from home, all represented welcome opportunities to bundle her little tribe off to that deeply loved haven of repose. There, the children from Küsnacht would be welcomed by their grandmother, their Uncle Ernst, their Aunt Marguerite, and their cousins.

Sometimes Carl did accompany them, and in his capacity as father and uncle, he would take the initiative of organizing games on a large scale on the Ölberg grounds. Beneath the somewhat perplexed gaze of the other parents, he would lead the enthusiastic group of youngsters off to enjoy picaresque adventures or Indian exploits of his own invention. The children fell immediately under the spell cast by Carl's energy and imagination. He had a particular talent for creating mystery and building up suspense, manifestly enjoying these games quite as much as did the children for whose benefit he supposedly organized them. These were truly happy moments of relaxation and deep harmony within the family.

Carl Jung and Ernst Homberger were brothers-in-law who may have had little in common but who nonetheless felt for one another a tremendous respect. Ernst's enlightened management of the watch factory brought in a very good income for the whole family; Carl, once a year, wrote to Ernst expressing his gratitude for the comfortable existence he was able to enjoy thanks to his brother-in-law's devotion to the family firm. There were, in other words, moments such as these, when happiness continued to bubble up to the surface as if by magic in the form of simple gestures of pleasure and appreciation.

At the beginning of 1914 Jung began to experience nightmares. Did these dreams of catastrophe prefigure the possibility of a nervous breakdown during this period when Jung's confrontation with the unconscious was still in full flood? The events that followed, the terrible and dramatic sufferings of World War I, subsequently enabled Jung to put his finger on the extent to which his dreams had informed him about happenings that were by no means merely subjective but that had taken on a fearful reality in the objective world. This personal experience confirmed Jung's belief in the existence of a collective unconscious. In a premonitory mode, his intuition had taken on board these tragic images of which he became the transmitter, the pained and pain-delivering messenger.

The Jungs' fifth and last child, their daughter Helene, was born in March 1914. Agathe, their eldest child, had already entered her tenth year. It seems clear that the couple considered their family to be complete at this point. How then were they to reconcile the legitimate desire for continuing intimacy and lovemaking with their fear of the possible consequences? Emma and Carl were still young and faced with the need to find some kind of a solution to this problem. What birth control measures could they take?

Their dilemma was, of course, a collective problem of their time, a difficulty to be viewed in the context of all the rules, limitations, and taboos that characterized these early years of the twentieth century. As for so many other couples keen to achieve a balanced and harmonious family life, there simply was no good solution. One radical but frequently adopted tactic was commonly referred to as "sleeping in separate beds" or "no longer sharing a room."

Taking into account the nature of both their workloads, along with respect for their differing needs and, almost certainly, other unspoken considerations, the couple reached the conclusion that they should sleep apart, a decision that must inevitably have entailed a decrease in intimacy. This "mutually agreed" new arrangement can only have been little more than the lesser of two evils.

It is hard not to conclude that, in this as in so many similar cases, the lack of any satisfactory alternative was what led to, or at any rate encouraged, the pursuit of extramarital sexual relationships. Jung's working hours were increasing in proportion to his growing fame and reputation as it spread across frontiers and oceans and reached the other side of the Atlantic. The children were thus ordered to keep quiet whenever they approached his office or were playing in the garden area just outside its window. The children's need to share the small everyday excitements of their lives was not always a weighty enough consideration in the face of Carl's demand for respect of *his* need to remain immersed in his solitary inner world even during family activities and mealtimes. It was Emma's constant duty to play the role of diplomat responsible for negotiations designed to reconcile the needs of the various members of the family. In this capacity, it was undoubtedly not pleasant for her to have to plead with her own children to speak more quietly, to be the one forced to silence their singing or their laughter. Even the family's pet dogs came in for their fair share of reprimands.

The long hours spent by Carl in voluntary reclusion and consultation with his patients in his library had a tendency to overflow into the wider family environment. Mealtimes were events of great importance for Carl, who was decidedly a gourmet, and when the situation or Dr. Jung's own mood so required, everyone at table was expected to observe complete silence, just as if the house were a monastery. At other times, when he was feeling relaxed, Carl would tell stories or recount his memories of the past, and such tales would frequently take on epic proportions. On these occasions, it was no longer forbidden to express emotions, and some rays of sunshine thus entered the family dining room.

The children, given this situation, became accustomed to looking principally to their mother as the parent with whom they sought to communicate. It was Emma who tended to their daily needs and answered their questions. She was stimulated by the need to keep up with their school studies, and the numerous subjects on the curriculum, whether literary or scientific, indeed contained few secrets for Emma. Carl G. Jung, as a father, wished for his children to remain quite free to make their own educational choices. But when decisions had to be taken, it was the upbringing and education that Emma had received that frequently served as the yardstick or model. Traditional values, implicitly, were applied or naturally transmitted themselves to her children. As a result of Emma's ingrained sense of elegance, the life of the whole family was imbued with an atmosphere of calm, refinement, and harmony.

It must not be forgotten that higher education at the beginning of the twentieth century still remained virtually closed to women. It is difficult for us nowadays to imagine that the range of opportunities open to girls at the time could really have been so very narrow, that the force of misogyny should for so long have retained its subtle hold. Switzerland was a particularly rigid country, and thus resistant to any form of social change.[13] That Emma herself had suffered on this count is a reasonable supposition but not something of which we have any definite proof. The restrictions that had affected her education remained applicable to her daughters. The *gymnasium* for girls in Zürich did not open until 1913, on the eve of World War I.

Agathe seemingly expressed no objection to this model and opted for marriage at the age of twenty. Gret did express opposition to the enforced segregation and, of the four daughters, was the only one to complete the four-year program of high school studies leading to the award of a higher school-leaving certificate. She subsequently went on to gain a specialized knowledge of astrology.

Franz, after a failed beginning in medical school, decided to study architecture well away from Zürich. In spite of Jung's pride in his only son, their characters were very different, and they rarely shared the same interests. Carl Gustav stated that Franz was very close to his mother. The children were somewhat in awe of their father, and his sudden bursts of anger were a constant source of fear in the family. At the same time, in his more relaxed moments, Carl was very often present and took pleasure in leading expeditions into the mountains, proposing cruises on the lake by sailboat, and inventing a wide assortment of games born of his fertile imagination. He thus contributed an element of fantasy to his children's lives, an attitude which Emma, concerned above all with maintaining harmony and balance within the family, probably did not allow herself to adopt.

As time went on, and especially from the beginning of Jung's confrontation with the unconscious, Toni Wolff's visits became increas-

13. The beginning of any true revolution in this respect did not come until the end of World War II. We forget all too easily that Swiss women were not officially granted the right to vote until 1971.

ingly frequent. She would come to see Jung in his office almost every day and often spend time with the family at other moments, too. By 1913 or 1914 Carl and Toni had recognized the depth of their attraction to one another, and the ensuing emotional triangle was to endure for decades.

This outside presence was a source of incomprehension and, to some extent, aggressiveness on the part of the children, who clearly were under an obligation to show her affection. As time went on, they came to sense that her presence within the family constituted an affront to their mother. Franz, above all, felt anger toward his father and habitually took his mother's side. Emma, quite naturally, appreciated the fact that her children wished to defend and protect her.

All commentators on this situation would agree, in any case, both that it was tremendously complicated and that it caused deep pain. It is unthinkable that there could have been any open discussion of it in the family, for subjects such as this were completely taboo. It has been suggested, however, that Jung may have opened up somewhat to his teenage daughters and spoken of the ambivalence of his own situation, his purpose in so doing having allegedly been to preserve these young women from an excessively idealized vision of the father. In choosing to speak of his urge to share his love between two women, he intended to convey the complexity of fully espousing his human condition (see Hannah 1976, 119).

Emma's external expression of serenity was undoubtedly a mask. It is not difficult to imagine the inner storms that must have raged on account of the almost daily episodes entailed by this painfully problematic coexistence. While there can be no doubt that Jung remained truly attached to his wife, he appears to have remained insensitive to the depth of the distress his behavior was causing her. It may be that he simply chose to ignore it, for the irresistible nature of his attraction apparently gripped him in a manner that was all-embracing and nonnegotiable. The mystery of the unconscious life of the psyche was here revealed in full daylight. Jung's feminine side, earlier lying dormant in this emotional sphere of his psyche, rushed forth to impose its presence.

What were Emma's feelings as she watched her husband and Toni Wolff descending the fine central staircase of her own home, animatedly exchanging the final sentences of a private conversation before Carl approached the family table for a meal? What else could she have felt but legitimate anger, bottomless despair, a profoundly threatening sense of existential anguish?

Let us pause here for a few moments and allow our imagination to range over a few scenes that might have been enacted by the couple in living out this deeply complex and highly delicate situation.

Carl Gustav comes down from his office at the end of his working day. He appears not to be in the best of moods. Indeed, he looks distinctly angry. He has seen one patient so lacking in understanding that he felt quite powerless to help him. After that, there was another woman whose constant flight from her unconscious also had the effect of freezing his ability to respond. Then he had found himself unable to fathom the meaning of some sections of a Latin text on alchemy, a failure that caused him additional frustration and annoyance. In short, today he's had as much as he can reasonably take.

Emma, too, has had a hard day. She came up against some difficulties in her research on the Holy Grail. Earlier she had spent some time helping her daughter who was at her wits' end over her math homework. Later in the afternoon, two of Jung's pupils came to her beset by anxieties over an assignment they had been given. Thanks to her own grasp of the subject, she managed to help them see the light. Her morning had been spent dealing with the servants' wages and orders for the household supplies for the coming weekend. All in all, Emma's day has been pretty exhausting.

*Over a cup of tea, Carl Gustav complains of deep
weariness. A lion, after all, is not meant to be kept
locked up in a cage. He really needs to get away for
a while. A change of air will enable him to recharge
his batteries, and for a long time he's been keen to
return to Florence. They have friends there who have
issued an open invitation. Why don't they accept? For
him the time is right. What bliss to contemplate the
incomparable artistic treasures of Florence! What does
Emma think? Why shouldn't they leave more or less
immediately?*

*Emma has promised to give a lecture at the Psychology
Club, which she still has to prepare. Her mother needs to
talk to her about something rather urgent. The children
have a few days off school, and she has promised that
they can invite some friends to stay. Emma cannot
decide to up and leave just like that. She has numerous
commitments in the home.*

*Well, if that's how it is, if Emma really isn't free
to accompany him just at the moment, Carl does not
mind going alone. Even better, he will ask Toni whether
she fancies coming with him. Emma, stunned and
wounded to the quick by this unexpected and brutal
announcement, is completely thrown and utterly
speechless. Had Carl Gustav stopped for one moment to
consider his wife's desires or feelings?*

*Shaken up and quite incredulous, Emma is
wondering what she has done to no longer merit Carl
Gustav's love and respect. A minefield of contradictions
and doubts is flooding her mind. Emma is overcome by
pain, anger, and despair, as well as by the intense fear
of abandonment. Even if it is Carl who is in the wrong,
any mention of her own anguish is likely to trigger
his wrath.*

How many wounding incidents or situations of this kind did Emma have to endure during these difficult and unpleasant years? Even if she possessed the understanding to realize that her husband's need for his relationship with Toni had its roots in his unconscious psyche, it was Emma who suffered the consequences. Even if Carl never once considered leaving his wife, this double life, this demand that she share her husband's time and affection with another woman, was sheer torture for Emma. If Carl's priority was to nourish his soul thanks to his relationship with Toni, did he really imagine that for Emma this mode of coexistence was tenable?

At a seminar on children's dreams given in 1939–1940, Jung developed associations to a specific dream image that dealt with the role of woman and of the anima for man:

> The anima as a friend or *soror mystica* has always played a great role in history. In the *cour d'amour* of René d'Anjou, she even takes precedence over the wife . . . . That's why the man projects his anima on to a suitable woman who shows some male characteristics. (Jung 2008, 321)

What is interesting and significant here is that if Jung had fallen prey to his anima, he was obviously not completely unaware of the fact. In his role as lecturer, he knew very well what he was talking about and was able to expound upon and amplify his subject while at the same time setting himself apart from the type of situation he was describing. Such was the deeply puzzling ambiguity of Carl's behavior.

Emma's feelings toward Toni, though rarely apparent on the surface, were characterized by no ambiguity whatsoever. While acknowledging Toni's intellectual stature and powers of intuition and perceiving that it was Carl's need for precisely these qualities that drew him to her, Emma was quite incapable of showing any affection toward her rival. How was she to feel anything but deep resentment at this woman's intrusion into her marriage and family life? Emma's pain, shame, and embarrassment were such that these feelings more than once caused her to renounce inviting her family to her home as she had previously been accustomed to doing. There was no way in which she could openly oppose Carl. His determination to follow his own needs, his own instincts, meant that he was completely deaf to any form of compromise.

What is to be said about Carl Gustav's own inner conflict? It is surely quite impossible to believe that he failed to take the measure of the deep pain he was inflicting on his wife. Whatever considerations he entertained in his own mind by way of justification cannot have prevented the always-present shadow of his infidelity from tarnishing the glass of trust and shared pleasure in relations with his wife. Even if Carl, in his own mind, was truly convinced that he continued to put his wife first and regarded her, above all, as the steadfast guardian of his family hearth, and even if their marital relations never actually came to a standstill, Carl had nonetheless thrust a dagger into his wife's heart.

Emma's ultimate response was silence. The decision to close in upon herself constituted her only means of moving forward. A deeply intelligent woman, she gradually found her own way of meeting the unnatural challenge represented by the enforced abandonment of all hope of once again becoming the only woman in this man's heart. This way forward led Emma to achieve a form of personal accomplishment, an inner liberation, an impressive maturity of the psyche. The remainder of our tale is an account of this gradual evolution.

There exist testimonies according to which Jung, during his long stay in Africa between 1925 and 1926, dreamed of this triangular relationship that he had put in place. What could be better proof that, contrary to appearances, he was haunted by the questions raised by his behavior? While Toni inundated him with letters, he expressed concern that Emma wrote so infrequently. Did he ever stop to consider what a heavy additional workload his prolonged absence imposed on his wife?

Whatever the nature and extent of his inner conflict on this score, Jung firmly refused to give up the relationship with Toni. Rather, he chose to accept as a necessary given what he experienced as his need for the fascination exerted by this brilliant mind, for the purity of the intuition represented in female form by the particular woman Toni Wolff. History, written from a male standpoint, frequently turns upon this eternally recurrent premise, described often in the form of myth and rendered in poetry and other forms of expression through which the pull of the anima is somehow enacted. The male, in other words, has a vital need for his muse, for the beauty that he finds flowing into his soul thanks to the *femme inspiratrice*. Insofar as there have always been women who appear destined to meet this need in men, it may be regarded as an arrangement that can work out well for both parties. In other words, it can suit everyone—everyone, that is, except the wife who has been sidelined, the woman whose love and devotion a husband makes light of, whether or not he goes so far as to cast her off or out. Such situations invariably give rise to intense pain; in some cases the outcome is a *drame passionnel*.

Emma retained her dignity and withstood the situation. She accepted—since she was not in a position to refuse—that Jung should choose to attend numerous gatherings in the company of two women, and that on some occasions he preferred to be accompanied by Toni alone. It was very hard for Emma not to experience at times a sense of her own inadequacy in the face of her husband's ever-increasing eminence. Although she had spoken to Freud of her anxiety in this respect, he had failed to appreciate the full extent of Emma's distress and bewilderment. Fortunately, she was well aware that she did truly matter to Carl and that, in society's terms, her position as his wife could not be called into question. She was able to treasure the memory of the early days of their expressions of mutual love and of the time when Carl had enthusiastically involved her, more than any other person, in his research and progress in the new science that he was discovering and tentatively exploring. Emma continued to derive great benefit from all that she had learned through this experience and from the way in which it had lastingly deepened and enriched her personality. Yet she now had no choice but to turn inward upon herself and to seek access to her own potential, to set out to discover the as yet unconscious and relatively undeveloped territories of her own personality.

The sense of having successfully brought up her children enabled Emma to emancipate herself gradually from the role of nurturing mother and to recover an area of freedom in her life. She took advantage of this situation to develop her independence and her personal intellectual pursuits. On the one hand, Jung had by this time begun to send her patients; on the other, she engaged the services of a teacher to satisfy her keen desire to further her knowledge of Greek and Latin. Carl encouraged his wife in these pursuits. It is indeed on record that he once told an analysand that it had been important for Emma to become an analyst for her personality had been far too centered on motherhood, she had been "too much of a mother woman" (Cabot Reid 2001, 128).

From this point on, Emma's remarkable maturity and spirit of generosity were what earned her the unswerving respect of the men and women who formed the inner circle of Jung's admirers and disciples. Strengthened and supported by the values she held dear, Emma slowly began to transcend a complex situation by working on it silently and inwardly. As soon as her youngest child, Helene, began school, Emma stepped up her studies. In 1916 she began to give lectures at the Psychology Club. Almost as a matter of course, she gradually entered professional practice as an analyst, seeing her patients under the same roof as Carl. Each had a consulting room on the first floor, and their respective analysands would attend their appointments by climbing the majestic staircase lit by the light from the large windows in the entrance tower.

This long stretch of the Jungs' family life was punctuated by innumerable events and developments. Both Emma and Carl lost their mothers. It was Emilie's death that triggered Jung's decision to construct what was to become the Bollingen Tower. Between 1916 and

1920 Emma was president of the Psychology Club. Both Carl and Emma traveled, sometimes together, sometimes separately.

From the United States, to which he had first traveled with Freud in 1909, Jung sent Emma letters in which he enthused about life in America and said that he hoped they would return there together one day. Curiously this sudden enthusiasm had caused Emma some disquiet, which she alluded to in one of her letters to Freud. Yet she subsequently accompanied him to the United States and derived much enjoyment from the trip.

A sudden and intense desire for travel was something that periodically seized Jung, attributable perhaps in part to the desire to put his intuitions on the collective unconscious to the test in other civilizations under the conditions of radically different cultures. At the same time, it was a means of gaining some relief from his relentless workload and probably also of escaping temporarily the awkward and tiresome aspects of daily life at Küsnacht. His first major expedition entailed a six-month stay in Central Africa in 1925, returning through Upper Egypt and via Cairo down the Nile. He wrote his first impressions to Emma: "This Africa is incredible. Unfortunately, I cannot write coherently to you, for it is all too much" (Jung 1961, 371).

Emma sent simple replies to such letters, supplying Carl with news of the family. The messages from this mother of five with the responsibility for running a large household undoubtedly lacked lyrical sophistication and may well have seemed mundane. Emma was the first to admit that she did not have her husband's fine literary style or epistolary talent. While Carl was amassing his memorable travel impressions, Emma was keeping the family and household running smoothly and managing her husband's professional affairs in his absence.

During this period Emma's various activities were intense. She was by now in her forties, and her children were growing up, with the youngest ones nonetheless still demanding a good deal of her attention. In this situation she did her best to combine her new work as a professional therapist with her family and social duties.

Emma was particularly sensitive to her immediate surroundings and to the needs of the persons around her. That her home was filled, thanks to her presence and caring efforts, with an atmosphere of both comfort and peace is an achievement to which her grandchildren still testify today. While Carl was chasing his intuitions and the impulses surging up from his unconscious, he left to the mistress of the hearth the heavy responsibility of overseeing all household concerns. At the end of the 1920s Jung set out on his second major expedition, this time to visit the Pueblo Indians of New Mexico. Then, some years later, he was unable to resist the fascinating pull of India.

As the years passed and his children became young adults, Carl was well able to perceive the rich and deeply precious nature of the family that he and Emma had created together. He enjoyed sharing his own interests and discoveries with the different members of his family, and he knew how to attune his speech and manner to the age and character of whichever one of them he was addressing. Emma, for her part, was the subtle advocate of her own primary values: respect for others, discretion, fidelity, the importance of the family, and the need to pay attention to developing and cultivating the mind. The five children thus derived great benefit from each of the two sources that flowed toward them from their parents, from these two exceptional and complementary personalities who enabled them to find their own secure anchorage while at the same time learning to open their minds and spirits to the wider world.

They were deeply influenced, undoubtedly, by their mother's unerring tenacity in preserving, through all the vicissitudes, her sense of fidelity to her commitments. While the underlying meaning of Emma's attitude may have been mysterious and the cause of recurrent pain, their mother's conviction concerning the essential and irreplaceable nature of her task and role cannot have escaped the children. Without openly expressing their feelings, they undoubtedly shared her moments of perplexity and anger. They were exposed also to their father's intuitions, to his bold visions of the symbolism of the so-called occult sciences and of alchemy. These children, in the future, were to be associated in differing ways with the development of the thought that became known as "Jungian"' and with some of the varying manifestations of its significance.

Agathe had played the role of a second mother for her two younger sisters, Marianne and Helene. At a still young age she unhesitatingly exchanged this responsibility for marriage, followed by her own long and peaceful family life. In middle life, she became an important source of warmth and support for her aging parents. Agathe died in 1998, age ninety-four, leaving an impressively large number of direct descendants.

Franz made his career as an architect. He helped his father draw up the plans for the alterations to and enlargement of the Bollingen Tower, and it was he who took over the house at 228 Seestrasse after his father's death in 1961. Surrounded by his wife, who died before him, and his four sons, he took chief responsibility for the family legacy until his own death at the age of eighty-eight. Serving in this way as the most direct and immediate link with his parents, he allowed the visitors he welcomed to his home to hear the still audible echo in the rooms of the great house in which Emma and Carl had brought up their large family.

Gret, whose independent nature and determination to do something different with her life made her reluctant to accept rules that she felt others sought to impose upon her, married her childhood sweetheart, and the young couple lived for many years in France and had five sons. After her return to Switzerland, Gret practiced as an astrologer, a field in which her skills were appreciated and earned her considerable recognition.

Marianne agreed to supervise the publication of her father's work in Switzerland, from the time she turned thirty-five to her premature death in 1965, only four years after her father. Of the five children, it had been she who spent the most time with her father after he became a widower. Marianne left behind a husband and three children. Her great love had been music, and as a girl she played the grand piano in the large living room in Küsnacht, filling the house with the instrument's warm and melodious tones. Emma, too, on occasion played the same piano and also sang.

Helene, the youngest child, very early showed her lack of interest in formal study, expressing her wish to develop her natural taste for needlework. She refined her talents in Paris and London, and before her marriage, she opened a clothes and dressmaking shop in the old quarter of Zürich together with her sister-in-law, Franz's wife. Even at an advanced age, she continued to practice her talents in this sphere. Helene's husband had died when she was barely forty, and after his death she began writing, becoming known for her research on the symbolism of icons. Having reached the age of one hundred, Helene was the last living member of Emma's immediate family, full of memories and offering a direct connection to this long family odyssey begun in 1904.

Helene Hoerni-Jung kindly agreed to write down some of her earliest and most tender childhood memories of her mother:

> My mother shared her husband's interests and would converse regularly with him on these subjects in a lively but also sometimes critical manner. With strangers she was restrained and somewhat retiring. She gave much time, attention, and understanding to answering our questions and dealing with our problems. There was little in the way of prohibition. In actual fact, she generally left the final decision up to us, after having first let us know her own opinion on the matter. My mother's opinions have always been very important to me. She appeared to us as a woman able to marshal an intelligent argument and full of ideas. This is somewhat surprising, in that she was also occasionally overcome by bouts of uncertainty. (Personal communication from Hoerni-Jung, December 2008)

This youngest daughter, invariably referred to as Lill by friends and family, added that while her mother was not very keen on housework, she prided herself on providing a welcoming and attractive table. The center of family life was a large room overlooking the garden and the lake. This was where they would have their meals all together; the dogs were never far away, and it was the room for schoolwork, festive occasions, receptions for prestigious guests, and family games of cards, even in adulthood. Helene recalled that "in the evening Mother and Father would both be absorbed in their complicated games of patience."

This moving testimony seems to confirm the impression that the children were particularly deeply imbued with their mother's values. These values constituted the set of references that influenced the life choices of this first generation. While their father's approach was observed with interest, the example of his complex marital situation apparently inspired his children to prefer other models.

This picture of a lively and fulfilling family life, full of openminded and enriching exchange, is further confirmed by the testimonies of several persons who were closely associated with Jung during this period. The biography of Godwin Peter Baynes, written by his younger daughter, and Barbara Hannah's memoir reveal many additional facets of the vitality and appeal that characterized the Jung family's daily life (Baynes Jansen 2003; Hannah 1976).

The family as a whole was, of course, affected by the restrictions and deprivations associated with World War II. The son and sons-in-law were conscripted into the army; all feared a German invasion, and several family members took refuge for a few weeks or even months in the mountains. They experienced shortages, bans on movement, and the forced return of Gret and her four children to their home in France; and they showed concern for the less-privileged people around them.[14]

---

14. All citizens with a garden were asked by the government to cultivate it in order to produce their own food. The Jung family followed this directive and turned its beautiful green parkland into a vegetable plot. The national authorities, at the same time, opened up collective spaces for the cultivation of cereals to cope with the rationing imposed.

Their gaze inevitably extended beyond the immediate frontiers of Switzerland to the terrible upheavals that were causing such suffering in neighboring countries. Zürich was bombarded in 1940. In April 1944 the Americans bombarded Schaffhausen by mistake, giving rise to deep concern about the family members still living there. The family at Küsnacht were well aware that their own fate was enviable in comparison to that of many others in situations of greater danger. In spite of all the pressures and the fears, they were able to preserve their freedom and offer hospitality to numerous refugees.

Jung took advantage of this period when travel was difficult to focus on his writing. It was at this time that the young Marie-Louise von Franz became his associate for the research on *Psychology and Alchemy* and *Mysterium Coniunctionis*. Alchemy was an area in which Toni Wolff, ill at ease with its traditionally occult and "diabolical" connotations, had declined to take an interest.

While the deep bond between them remained, the relationship between Jung and Toni evolved significantly over the years. Jung's need had been met. The view expressed by one member of his inner circle was that Carl had drunk of Toni's soul to the very dregs. It surely is the case that Toni also derived tremendous benefit from the association. Yet if one chooses to embark on the path of imagining her doubts, anxieties, and inner conflicts, it will surely become apparent that the intensity of the relationship must have caused her as much suffering as it did joy. After a number of years, she did her best to gain some distance from such intense proximity. Toni also became a well-known analyst of high repute to whom Jung referred a large number of patients who invariably benefited from her exceptional intuition.

While she seems to have been a woman with little taste for physical relationships, Toni Wolff was endowed with a very special charm and numerous admirers came under her spell. She never married and continued to live with her mother until the latter's death. Having previously gained a reputation as something of a spoiled child and a recluse, during World War II she surprised everyone by accepting a volunteer job as a driver and assistant with the women's

aid corps, the *Frauenhilfsdienst*. She devoted herself wholeheart-
edly to this work in spite of suffering chronic pain caused by rheumatoid arthritis.

With the passage of time, Emma's hostile feelings toward Toni
became tempered and lost some of their bitterness. The acute sting
of the pain had faded, even if an ache remained at the site of the
scars. The two women became united in a relationship that was
perhaps akin to friendship, albeit a friendship inevitably tinged by
memories of the former tactlessly enforced proximity that they had
experienced, more often than not, as a grueling promiscuity. The nascent friendship enabled them to serve a common cause, the cause
of depth psychology, of which for a long period they formed the
central core. Emma and Toni Wolff were able in the end, with the
help of an analyst, to tackle their conflicts and respective grievances
in a spirit of openness and sincerity, and to reach, finally, a peaceable outcome. Emma came to feel compassion for a woman who had
known the joys neither of a home nor of a family, whose vocation
had lain in another sphere of relationship.

This outcome is indeed a tribute to the courage of which women
can show themselves capable. What heights of abnegation must have
been required for these two women to succeed in facing up to the
fraught issues and extreme complications that had built up between
them over thirty years of rivalry. Emma's nobility of soul and fundamental generosity led her to ask whether rivalry was indeed the
only possible outcome of the situation in which she had been placed
or whether she might perhaps be able to move beyond her feelings
of jealousy. To transform the guilt feelings associated with jealousy,
to accept responsibility for these feelings, and to accept the need to
share her love for her husband added up to a sublime task such as is
described in myths. Emma explored this subject in a lecture entitled
"Schuld," which she gave at the Psychology Club as early as 1916.[15]
The choice of title must surely be read as a sign that this vastly com-

---

15. The German abstract noun can translate into English as "fault," "blame," or "guilt."

plex topic had been at the heart of Emma's preoccupations from an early stage in her difficulties.

In 1944 Carl Gustav Jung suffered a dangerous blow and threat to his health. For several years he had been afflicted with an intestinal disorder caused by the presence of amoebae contracted during his visit to India. As he had preferred to ignore this condition rather than seek treatment, his complaint had weakened him and brought about weight loss. A fall during a walking trip caused a fracture to his ankle, on account of which he was taken to the hospital and confined to bed. The resulting immobility brought on incipient phlebitis, a pulmonary embolism, and finally a heart attack. From February until the end of June, Jung remained literally cloistered in a private clinic in Hirslanden, a suburb of Zürich, under Emma's constant and highly vigilant supervision.

For Jung this was a major life and life-threatening event. The heart attack caused him to fall into a coma. In the grip of these "intermediate" states, he saw visions that he regarded as the most important experiences of his whole life. During this period, Jung seemed to be under the influence of a death wish. His nearest and dearest, and in particular his wife, were plummeted into unutterable anguish by this distressing development. As Barbara Hannah, who knew the Jungs well at this time, testified, "It was naturally very difficult and painful for his wife to endure his ardent longing for death and the temporary cessation of his usual human warmth" (Hannah 1976, 281).

For Emma, who watched over her husband unceasingly, this situation provided, without any doubt, the opportunity to gather under her protective wing this man suffering the throes of a grave regression of both body and mind. These months of almost total reclusion were followed by a slow and painful return to reality.

Emma had decided that her husband, during these long weeks, should be kept beyond reach of the outside world. Virtually no one, other than his children, was allowed to come through the door. No news of his progress was forthcoming to the outside world. No communiqués were issued. Emma had herself moved into the clinic and did not leave it until her husband had recovered sufficiently to be able to return home.

The public man had been cast back into an exclusively private life. One of the very few persons admitted into his presence was Marie-Louise von Franz. Since she was involved in Jung's research on alchemy, Emma considered, toward the end of his convalescence, that such a visit might stimulate in her husband the desire to renew his grasp on the thread of life. Toni Wolff did not take kindly to being sidelined in this manner, for even though her relationship with Jung was undeniably no longer what it had been, the two nonetheless remained very attached to one another.

It was thus that 1944 marked an important turning point in the relationship between Carl and Emma as a couple and in the evolution of each of the marriage partners taken separately. Carl actually believed during this illness that he had reached the end of his life. His return to the land of the living caused a tempest of freedom to rage through his whole mind and being. He felt a strong conviction that the findings amassed over decades could now be assembled to produce works that would bear an increasingly personal stamp. Carl was by this time sixty-nine, while Emma was sixty-two. Each of them was gradually to embark on the search for a new kind of closeness with the other, for a matured form of love, and a friendship based on wisdom. Their earlier knowledge of romantic passion had been transformed through the white heat of suffering and long experience. It was now, perhaps, that the couple was in a position to look forward to a new golden age.

Carl's seventieth birthday was celebrated in private in July 1945, for the period of his official convalescence had not yet come to an end. Even so, he received gifts from the psychological community of Zürich. This now semi-institutionalized community was strongly attached to its founder and master, who drew along in his wake, with ever more forceful impetus and inspirational power, an increasingly large number of disciples.

Emma was able to return, almost unimpeded, to her personal research, her professional work as an analyst, and her watercolor experiments. She took great pleasure in the simple joys of being a grandmother who, having now witnessed the birth of her children's children, was able to watch a new generation grow up. Emma's grandchildren came to stay with her during their school holidays; she would go with them to the lake's edge to swim or, at other times, help them with their schoolwork. Emma, who had herself given birth to four girls and a boy, ended up with a total of fifteen sometimes frighteningly energetic and turbulent grandsons and four granddaughters. What happiness it must have been for her to be able to share her beautiful and wonderfully harmonious residence at 228 Seestrasse with this new generation of children and young people so full of vitality and for whom the door to the future was still wide open.

Today some of the grandchildren still reminisce about the family gatherings around the Christmas tree, with the gifts that Emma herself had so carefully chosen for each member of the family. As parents and grandparents, Carl and Emma Jung showed a truly impressive combination of generosity, intelligence, and sensitivity in the attention paid to each individual family member, and they created within their home traditions and festive atmospheres that left a strong and unforgettable imprint on all who took part.

It may be interesting at this point to remember the Latin motto that the couple had had engraved above the front door when they first moved into their Küsnacht residence:

VOCATUS ATQUE NON VOCATUS DEUS ADERIT
(Whether invited or not, God will be present.)

The sacred character of this family house had, in other words, been solemnly declared and built into the masonry from the outset.

Did this Latin inscription knowingly prefigure the many-hued shimmering and complex displays of life and vitality that would be enacted within the walls of this family home? The true lord of the house had here been recognized and named.

Serving as the lodestar of their long-term endeavor, the words engraved above the Jungs' front door would ultimately appear to have protected the family's frequently storm-tossed yet impressively fertile passage through their own generation and beyond. Their place of residence may truly be said to have been inhabited by the Spirit.

Before bringing this chapter to a close, let us stop for a moment to look at a particularly charming family portrait. On a sunny Sunday in 1917 the Jung family is enjoying an excursion to Château d'Oex. Before going into the restaurant for lunch, they pose for a photograph on their hotel terrace.

Carl is forty-two years old. Though dressed in a jacket and tie, his boots seem to suggest that a walk in the mountains is on the program for the day's activities. The children's boots tell us that his son Franz, age nine, and his daughter Marianne, age seven, are also to accompany him. Emma and the two older girls, Agathe and Gret, age thirteen and twelve, have seemingly chosen other activities. Emma is thirty-five. While her face is partially hidden by a hat, the finely chiseled line of nose and mouth are visible. The elegant dresses are in predominantly pale colors; the poses are extremely natural. This snapshot simultaneously tempts us to dream and brings a smile to our lips. Contemplating this picture, we feel that we learn a great deal about the fine-looking family enjoying a happy interlude in this mountain resort. Only the youngest child, Lill, is absent from the picture. A little girl of just three at the time, she may have been having her afternoon nap, or perhaps she did not accompany them on this particular outing.

Over and above the inevitable twists and turns of fate, the family manifestly found its own way of preserving what was most truly essential. The impression gained in relation to the lives and fortunes of Carl and Emma Jung's numerous children and grandchildren is that they indeed found, in the values handed down to them by their parents and practiced in their day-to-day lives, the prerequisites for their own continuing fulfilment. There can surely be no doubt whatsoever that Emma, on the scale of merit, deserved the very highest award.

6

.

Carl's and Emma's
Professional Commitments:
Zürich, Eranos, Travels

After an attempt to offer an overall picture of the Jungs' family life
through a series of vignettes, we now move on to consider the various facets, in Zürich and beyond, of the couple's social and professional involvement in the developing world of analytical psychology, its practice, and the first institutions to be set up. This is also an
appropriate place to mention the annual Eranos gatherings, which
rapidly gained a reputation as a crossroads for the exchange of ideas,
where many of the greatest minds of the twentieth century had the
opportunity to meet and share their discoveries. For Emma and especially Carl G. Jung, Eranos represented an extraordinarily refresh-
ing oasis for the enjoyment of new and wide-ranging ideas expressed
and exchanged in a spirit of deep and open intellectual freedom.

The very special position of C. G. Jung resulting from his chosen
profession and swiftly growing reputation exerted a powerful effect
on the life of his wife and family. This influence was particularly felt
by Emma, who by nature gave priority for quite a number of years
to her role as wife and mother. While her children were still young
Emma made every effort to shelter them from the turbulence, vi-

cissitudes, and polemics that marked the years of development and gradual institutionalization of the Jungian venture in Zürich and Küsnacht.

This need to protect her children from the repercussions of their father's notoriety represented, for Emma, a complex and challenging endeavor in a number of respects. The Jung children attended the local schools in Küsnacht and Zürich. As C. G. Jung's reputation grew, so did the rumors, reactions of assent or disapproval, and the gossip. He had his admirers, who tended more often than not to be female. For the women of his inner circle Jung was indeed something of a god. He also, however, had his detractors. He was believed by some to possess occult or magical powers, and he was accused by others of meddling in the affairs of the devil. This was, generally speaking, a source of amusement for Jung. His strength of character, sense of humor, and, above all, freedom of mind were perfectly able to accommodate such rumors. Nor did it displease him, at the other extreme, to be the subject of adulation.

The respectability of the Rauschenbach family, of whose great wealth and social rank no one in Switzerland could have remained unaware, was another dimension of the life of this microcosm; and Emma certainly had no wish to tarnish this image. She took good care, for example, to ensure that her husband was always appropriately attired, for to Emma dress was an important indicator of social prestige. To Carl, on the other hand, it was a matter of much less concern, and he felt distinctly more at ease in clothes favored by the type of man whose preference is to live close to nature rather than go about his business in the social world. His own choice of attire reflected his taste for manual labor. Working in stone and getting mud on his hands were second nature to Carl, who felt himself to be a creature of the mountains and experienced the need to remain in touch with the primitive man within. This was why Jung felt most at home at the tower he built in Bollingen.

Thus it was that the idiosyncratic behavior and newfangled ideas of the strange and unconventional Dr. C. G. Jung did not always sit quite comfortably with the preferences of the elegant Mrs. Jung, who cultivated a high degree of taste for conventional discretion, reserve, and social respectability. Emma, left to her own devices, would undoubtedly have preferred to devote much of her time to contemplation of her garden, reading, and the pleasures of the home.

The Jung children derived, in alternate measure, benefit or discomfort from one parent's reputation or the other. One of Emma's preoccupations was to preserve for her children access to the respectable bourgeois class into which she had been born and amid the values of which she had grown to adulthood. It is not unreasonable to assume that she hoped to raise girls who would be able to make good marriages within this society. To Emma's way of thinking, this was the means of ensuring that her daughters would enjoy a comfortable social and material life. She was a woman imbued with the traditional values of Switzerland, and her own family in Schaffhausen radiated an image of bourgeois affluence and influence combined with a genuine and deep-seated concern for the commonweal.

Emma's choices and preferences naturally prompt a whole host of questions. Impelled or encouraged by her mother, she had found herself propelled by her marriage to a young doctor from a modest background—but rich in terms of culture and ambition—into a world in the throes of a scientific revolution. One of the not necessarily intended but evident consequences of this choice was a shift in Emma's social position, away from the center ground represented by traditional bourgeois respectability to a less conventional and more peripheral area. Exposure to the striking personality of Jung could not but prompt Emma to question her adherence to some of the traditional values with which she had grown up, causing her to view the world, to some extent, with new eyes. The shock represented by the proximity to such an unusual, not to say eccentric, husband was compounded, moreover, by the peculiar dynamic of the psychological community within which he moved, for this was an environment that allowed—and, no doubt, virtually compelled—Emma to transgress some of her bourgeois values.

Emma was inevitably caught up in the wake of C. G. Jung's growing reputation, which constituted for her a strong force of attraction
and fascination. It was her own husband's growing fame that enabled
her to meet a whole series of prominent and extremely interesting
figures. In addition to Sigmund Freud, Albert Einstein had been a
visitor to the Jungs' home. The writers Hermann Hesse and James
Joyce, Richard Wilhelm, sinologist and translator of the *I Ching*,
the statesman Winston Churchill, accompanied by his wife and his
daughter, and many more eminent figures sought association with
Jung and, more often than not, met his wife also. Would Emma have
enjoyed such opportunities if she had remained tamely at home in
her native Schaffhausen?

While Emma initially did what she could to shelter her family circle from the intense social life that raged around them, as they grew
up the children enjoyed great freedom and were themselves in a position to derive benefit from these contacts. Emma's own attitudes
and behavior also evolved as her husband's position developed and
as a result of circumstances that enabled her to develop and assert
her own potential and talents.

That Emma chose to accept this delicate and uncomfortable position of constantly mediating between one social milieu and another
was, without any doubt, already a sign that her nature possessed the
strength and particular bent required to embark on such a great personal adventure. Emma was never afforded the leisure to rest; yet
she knew that, in her life alongside Carl Gustav Jung, she had found
an opportunity to deploy her own potential, to enrich the life of her
own mind, to explore the many dimensions of her own psyche, and
to play her part in the fascinating, subtle, and tentative progress of
the new science of analytical psychology and the mysteries of the
soul whose depths it sought to plumb.

What then were the most striking and recurrent features of
the Jungs' social and professional life in Zürich and above all in
Küsnacht? The Jung family had moved to Küsnacht in the summer
of 1909, and the principal locus of Jung's professional life and activ-

ity shifted with the move to this new home. The first floor of their large residence had been designed to contain, at its center, Jung's office, together with his rich library. Here also were the quarters reserved for the parents and the youngest children. The one paradoxical aspect of the design of this extremely spacious house was that the architect—and Jung, too, it seems—had forgotten to include in the plans a waiting room for patients arriving for their appointments. Accordingly, it was the so-called linen room on the first floor that came to serve this purpose, an improvised arrangement that was hardly to the taste of the mistress of the house. This single fact speaks volumes about Jung's own conception of his home, while Emma, it seems likely, had simply not been consulted on these matters.

Most of the analysands who came to consult Jung (the majority of them women, frequently from far away) stayed in the few hotels and guest houses in the vicinity. Many came from abroad—from Germany, Great Britain, the United States of America—sometimes staying many weeks or returning for appointments on a regular basis. Some even decided to take up permanent residence nearby. All these people, very cosmopolitan and undoubtedly all with interesting personal histories and many tales to relate, came into contact with one another, became acquainted with one another, and began to talk about themselves. The Jung residence thus provided, at one and the same time, the premises for therapy appointments and a venue for social contacts. It was an unprecedented experience. There were those who tired of this proximity, which could so easily tip over into promiscuity. Those present and involved in this milieu, in accordance with their respective situations and characters, judged the atmosphere in the vicinity of Jung's Zürich-based practice to be sometimes stimulating, sometimes disturbing, and sometimes decidedly stifling.

Jung's privileged relationship with Toni Wolff was an open secret. As soon as Jung considered Toni to have acquired the requisite skills to work as a therapist he entrusted some of his patients to her. This was the pattern according to which, over the years, several former patients or disciples who had attended Jung's seminars became ana-

lysts themselves. Toni Wolff and Emma Jung rapidly formed the ker-
nel of this new practice. Other men and women followed, joining
this inner circle, including Barbara Hannah, Jolande Jacobi, Peter
Baynes, Marie-Louise von Franz, Carl A. Meier, and a number of
others. This form of induction into the profession took place without any sort of formality other than Jung's own initiative or agreement. He was, for a very long time, the only one to grant access to
the position of therapist.

It was not rare for Jung, frequently in the company of his wife
and Toni, to come into contact with the men and women who were
his patients at receptions, restaurants, cultural gatherings, birthday
parties, or at the Psychology Club's annual carnival, which he himself had brought into existence. It was also a frequent occurrence
that Jung, in the course of an analytical session, was called upon to
interpret a dream about himself, his wife, or other persons present in
the immediate professional vicinity.

The bizarre quality of these social and professional juxtaposi-
tions did not escape Jung's notice. On the contrary, he found them
to be particularly valuable and did not object to such shifting and
multifaceted encounters insofar as they offered plenty of opportunities for the analysis of projections and to compare and contrast
the objective and subjective viewpoints of dream figures within the
context of this virtually closed microcosm. This particular form
of proximity endowed social contacts and the overall atmosphere
with a very special hue that it is difficult to imagine nowadays. It
is strangely reminiscent of a tightrope artist's act conducted in an
experimental hothouse!

Emma and Carl obviously occupied a central place in this small
world where everyone knew everything, or almost everything,
about everyone else. Emma knew and was known to all. Assisted
by a secretary, the tasks for which she took responsibility included
organizing appointments, filtering enquiries, and sending out letters. She was, in return, the subject of special personal expressions
of gratitude and would regularly receive gifts of flowers, chocolates,

or books. The new science of analytical psychology evolved in this laboratory where the emotional charge was intense; and this small group of people found itself transformed, little by little, into a community.

At the initiative of a few individuals, the Psychology Club was set up in 1916. Initially housed on the premises at first one location and then a second, the club finally settled at its present address, 27 Gemeindestrasse in Zürich. This is a large town residence, donated to the Jungian community by a generous American patron, Edith McCormick-Rockefeller. The club became and remains today a venue for meetings intended to convey the essence and content of Jung's teachings. From the time of its creation, the events organized there included lectures and seminars but also gatherings intended to provide entertainment.

Emma Jung was the Psychology Club's first official president, from 1916 to 1920. Her main reason for accepting this position was to avoid conflicts and rivalries among the different candidates. There were some whose ambition was titillated by the prospect of occupying this position and the power thereby conferred. Others deplored the dissensions and gossip generated within this hive of psychological industry while recognizing the value of the privileged and complementary relationships that were created there and represented its most enriching component.

From the moment of her appointment, Emma had to contend with the eddies and whirlpools characteristic of a young association still in search of its path. She took the initiative of asking each member to put in writing his or her expectations and concerns. To this end, Emma circulated a letter containing the following request:

> and so we are writing to ask all of you who are truly
> interested in the development of our club to send us
> your impressions, suggestions or criticism on matters of
> both principle and practice which might be put up for
> discussion.

A plenary meeting was convened to discuss the points raised in response to this letter. Emma Jung, summing up the situation, enumerated the principles most appropriate for forming the cornerstone of the nascent organization:

> In responding to such reactions it is essential to show understanding rather than to express criticism. If the club is not yet in a position to meet the great need for it that we believe exists, this does not mean that it cannot do so in the future. It will, in my opinion, find its rightful place in the course of time.... Development is not only a matter of each person becoming an individual in himself, but of his feeling, as an individual complete in himself, that he is also part of a larger unit; ... in the face of the difficulties, we can do no more than entrust ourselves fully to the goodwill of one another and to the power of correction and improvement that all of us carry within ourselves.

It is thus that Emma Jung—age thirty-four—marked with her personal stamp this newborn social and cultural association. Her wish was that the Psychology Club should become the mirror and the motor empowered to reveal the specificity of depth psychology and to drive forward its influence. She agreed to act as the mouthpiece of this organization because there was no doubt in her own mind that it would serve as a precious tool to promote and disseminate the many aspects of her husband's pioneering approach as it continued to forge its fruitful path into the future.

The Psychology Club offered the opportunity for its members to prepare lectures on subjects explored or developed by Jung himself. In this context, too, Emma was very ready to make her contribution, and from the beginning she expounded her personal research findings. Her first lecture was given during the first year, 1916, and its title, as mentioned in chapter 5, was "Schuld." An audience of some thirty analysts, analysands, foreign visitors, and doctors, both men and women, listened to Emma's lecture, which she delivered in a manner that was simultaneously clear, direct, profound, and personal. The subject chosen by Emma Jung for this first lecture was the experience and meaning of guilt. Her presentation, thoroughly grounded in a strong level of general knowledge, showed her to be equally at ease in the handling of specifically psychological concepts.

It is striking now to realize that the presentation given by Emma on this occasion is, above all, a profound reflection on the subject of guilt feelings. This raises the question of the extent to which its content can be read as an echo of the letter sent by Emma some years earlier to Freud concerning her distress at Carl's adventure with Sabina Spielrein. Did not Emma, in this lecture, give expression to the personal search that she had been compelled to conduct in order to overcome a situation that she had experienced as catastrophic? Had she not interpreted her struggle as a test imposed by destiny rather than as the outcome of personal fault?

The presentation comes back to the theme of the Grail which, as the reader is already well aware, was a research topic close to Emma's heart. One thing that this legend suggested to her is that failures encountered in life may be the consequence of excessive compliance with received ideas. The Grail accordingly can be reached only by accepting responsibility for one's failures and thereafter abandoning the traditional paths so as to avoid falling once again into the same ruts and experiencing the same pitfalls of destiny. It is impossible not to perceive a link with the attitude that Emma had been forced to devise and adopt in order to survive the impossible situation imposed by her husband. It is reasonable to assume that this presentation was addressed to an audience most of whom were acquainted with the nature of the difficulties that Emma herself faced. The courage, discretion, and sincerity that she demonstrated by speaking of her most intimate concerns in this way are quite astounding.

Over the years, Emma was to speak on other topics. There was the paper on animus and anima that she later turned into an essay. There were also, and above all, the subsequent stages in her research on the subject that most deeply exercised her mind, the Grail legend. Most of these texts are clearly written, stylistically pleasing, and couched in personal terms. For these reasons, it is to be hoped that they may one day be made available for publication and translation.

Jung, for his part, continued to deploy his energy and talents unerringly, utterly convinced that his many writings would suffice to ensure the survival of his concepts. From time to time, he bemoaned the fact that most of those who came to hear lectures at the club were, like the majority of his patients, women. By way of explanation, Jung himself suggested various but equally significant reasons, which it may be of interest to consider here insofar as they pertain also to the context in which Emma was living and the background against which she was thinking her thoughts.

It is important, first of all, to remember that World War I had massacred millions of men, leaving behind similar numbers of women prematurely widowed or fated to remain single. All of these women had to find ways of providing for themselves and were, by the same token, obliged to develop their independence. The route taken by many of them was development of their thinking function or, as Jung termed this creative activity of the mind, their *logos*. In view of the success encountered by Jung's thoughts among women, one is bound to conclude that analytical psychology indeed offers an approach particularly well suited to the female mind.

Another component of Jung's largely female audience were women of the bourgeoisie, rich heiresses, wives of businessmen, ladies with plenty of money, sometimes far in excess of their needs, and with time on their hands and accustomed to a fairly high level of culture but in search of a deeper personal interest or meaning in their lives. As the industrial age experienced its prime, there was no shortage of such women, many of whom came from the United States. Their names are those of some of the great transatlantic dynasties: Rockefeller, McCormick, Mellon, and many others. Jung attributed this influx of women to what he saw as specifically female psychological characteristics. Insofar as women had undergone less of a strict educational or vocational training, their minds were less closed, placing them in a better position to gain access to their depths. Men he saw as being much more anchored in their rational minds. This observation seems all the more pertinent when one bears in mind that analytical psychology draws its knowledge from the most mysterious sources of all—from the infinite ocean of the collective unconscious.

Woman, by virtue of her natural maternal function, the physiological bearer of new life, is perhaps more spontaneously inclined to question the mysteries of life. Jung noted further that it was most often through the woman or wife that the man or husband would, after a period of delay, succeed in developing a capacity for psychological sensitivity and curiosity. And it was undoubtedly better to arrive at this point late rather than never. Emma's life and experience, in any case, were located at the confluence of these various developments. She was led to take up and develop, on her own behalf, not one but several vocations.

Whether at Küsnacht or—albeit more selectively—at Bollingen, the Jungs were not sparing with their hospitality. Jung received patients and visitors in his office and library. But if the weather was clement, he would open his garden to his patients and conduct their analytical sessions there. Emma on occasion—as recollected by one guest—would bring out tea, as a gesture of habitual Swiss hospitality and refinement. On other occasions she would spend time with a patient awaiting an appointment who might have requested her personal opinion or advice on some particular matter. Meanwhile, Jung felt the need to escape to Bollingen at frequent intervals in order to recharge his batteries. Often he went alone, placing his tower explicitly out of bounds for others, although Toni Wolff was, for a long period, one of the rare persons admitted to visit him there.

Aware of the special position they occupied in the lives of their numerous friends, acquaintances, pupils, and associates, Emma and

Carl were always ready to attend ceremonies held to mark important events in the private lives of others. Whenever they were invited
to such gatherings, they would do their best to put in an appearance,
and they invariably brought with them their savoir faire, elegance,
affection, cheerful companionship, and simplicity. For example, as
World War II was raging beyond their frontiers, Carl and Emma
attended a "fine Swiss wedding," seeing it not as an escapist gesture,
but as an opportunity to experience friendship, solidarity, abundance, and the joys of life in the presence of the young newlyweds so
full of hope and trust in life (Cabot Reid 2001).

Both Emma and Carl were prolific correspondents. In Jung's
many letters, the intimate, compassionate, understanding, caring,
and generous man is frequently allowed to emerge. Emma, as we
know, chose not to bequeath her correspondence to posterity. The
few letters that escaped the flames reveal a woman simultaneously
respectful and concerned, enlightened and devoid of pretension.
Emma would express her joy at a birth, her condolences at a death,
or her concern on the occasion of sickness. No letter sent to either
Carl or Emma ever remained unanswered. If there was any delay in
replying, an apology would be given. All correspondents were deserving of the same respect, no matter whether they were eminent
scholars or unknown patients.

On the occasion of a birth, Emma sent her congratulations:

Dear Mrs. Cabot!

Our very best congratulations for this happy event,
the arrival of your grandson! I hope it will bring much
joy and happiness also into your life: it is so nice to be
in contact with new, young life through one's children
and grandchildren! I am looking forward to seeing you,
and to hearing how you feel about your new dignity.
(Cabot Reid 2001, 454)

However simple the terms in which they are couched, such messages convey a sense of sincerity deriving from Emma's own experience as mother and grandmother.

Carl reserved his bursts of anger or irony for his nearest and dearest who, on occasion, fell prey to a wounding sarcasm, the intention behind which was not always apparent. When his youngest daughter announced to him, at the age of forty, that she intended to begin writing, Carl apparently retorted that this was a "very peculiar idea" for a person destined to spend her life "wielding saucepans and dusters." What is one to make of this disrespectful treatment of the woman? Was it an expression of utter surprise on her father's part? Or could his intention have been to put his daughter's determination to the test?

If people from outside the family made a nuisance of themselves, Jung knew very well how to protect himself or hold his ground. Snobs who took pleasure in teasing or taunting him were met with irony and Jung's irrefutable and stinging wit, which, according to Schopenhauer, is man's sole divine quality.

In response to men and women who came to him with their doubts and hesitations, the trivial or overwhelming causes of their distress, Jung adopted the attitude of a caring father, a steadfast patriarch, displaying a quite remarkable capacity for patience. He knew that it was on the quality of his listening that he would be judged, and he spared himself no pains and supplied endless examples and associations, together with mythological or alchemical amplifications. He was fully convinced that these were an effective part of the treatment insofar as they opened up the mind and led not only to understanding but, even more importantly, to the experience of meaning. Since Emma was in Carl's presence on a daily basis, she was accustomed and attentive to her husband's mood swings, whether in the family or the professional setting, and she never hesitated to comment as she thought appropriate or to seek to offer tactful remedy where necessary.

Emma was deeply imbued with all that she had gleaned over the years from her husband, starting in the earliest years of their marriage. Scrupulously, she took active steps to further and refine her analytical apprenticeship, and she had been immersed for so many years in the crucible of this flourishing new science that it ultimately came to seem that she was in a perfectly natural position, with her well-developed sense of vigilance, to serve others as a guide in their course of descent into the depths of the unconscious, which can lead to the discovery of the Self and activate the processes of individuation.

Encouraged by Carl, Emma decided that the time was now ripe to offer her skills as a therapist. Her youngest daughter had started school, and her maternal duties were therefore less all-consuming. Jung was delighted because he was himself totally overburdened by a constantly growing clientele, so he referred patients to Emma. He knew her intelligence, her integrity, her intuition. He knew how long and hard she had worked to acquire the knowledge that she now possessed. He saw her as a "faultless dove," both centered and grounded.

In this house that was well and truly the heart and hearth of her life, Emma set up an office of her own on the first floor. She created and stocked her own library at the back of the house so that her professional quarters, like Carl's, had a view of the garden and the lake. It was here that Emma carried out her research and developed her professional activity as a therapist. Her practice was much appreciated and she garnered much respect. Her therapeutic approach was grounded in her primary sensation function, seconded by a solid feeling function. Over the years, in contact with Carl, Emma had also developed her intuition function.

Emma's patients were reassured by her attitude of welcoming concern and benefited from the subtly attuned quality of her listening, which undoubtedly owed much to her own experience of severe inner turmoil and the power of such storms to transform the psyche. One of her analysands was Peter Baynes, who had previously been in analysis with Jung and had subsequently become a close friend and associate. He chose to consult Emma when he found himself in a state of turmoil on account of marital uncertainties. He needed to make a decision: Should he move toward divorce, or might he consider conducting two relationships concurrently? This was the circumstance that enabled him to elicit Emma's human and therapeutic response on the occasion of their meeting. He wrote his impressions in his diary:

> Emma was just lovely. We just seemed to get to a calm leisurely mood like a broad river where we found the most human understanding. She told me lots of things about herself . . . and she said, "You see Peter, I would never say that the way things are in our lives (meaning Toni and C. G.) is in any way a solution." She let me know how she had suffered and how she still suffers. (Quoted in Baynes Jansen 2003, 251)

Following this exchange Peter was able to emerge from his state of tension, conflict, and indecision and to conclude that his being divided between two women was the cause of intense suffering for all concerned and could ultimately represent a solution for none of them. Jung had reached a different conclusion which, indeed, had spared no one and had, on the contrary, been the cause of inner torment for each member of the triangle in question. In such a paradoxical and chronically painful situation can there be any single right answer?

In comparison with the Jungs' life in Küsnacht, Bollingen offered the possibility of seclusion. The "secret refuge" that Jung had built for himself there was the privileged location to which he retired when he wished to spend time writing, working on his mural paintings, or carving in wood or stone. Emma, too, was pleased to have such a place to relax, even if the early rudimentary facilities and lack of comfort were not precisely to her taste. In this and many other situations, Emma may be said to have displayed a preparedness to give and take that was truly legendary in its proportions: "adapt elegantly and complain seldom" would seem to have been her personal motto. In the course of time, spells at Bollingen came to represent for the couple the opportunity to spend time away from their everyday pursuits and duties in a secret and intimate place far from the public gaze. The years passed and, as the place became better equipped with home comforts, they would spend increasingly long periods there. Gradually even Emma came to speak of the place as "our beloved Bollingen."

Jung had begun to build his tower in 1923 after his mother's death. The round tower, which he built with his own hands and the help of local masons, fulfilled the crucial function of signifying the return to the original mother under the protection of the spirits. Jung stated that living close to nature, drawing water from the well, cutting his own wood, and walking on natural stone floors was for him a way of reconnecting with primitive origins and linking up with the Self. While the original tower was enlarged and gradually made more comfortable, he did not actually complete the construction until after Emma's death in 1955.

It was at Bollingen that Jung wrote several of his important works, including *Aion* and *Psychology and Alchemy*. Emma also took advantage of the calm and solitude of the tower to prepare various lectures to be given at the Psychology Club or at the C. G. Jung Institute, which was set up many years later, and to continue her research on the Grail. This work, in which she had first become interested during her early youth, was still in gestation. And, work aside, Bollingen provided a venue for spending intimate moments with one or another member of the family. The Jungs invited their children and grandchildren to spend time there with them, one or a few at a time, and such an invitation was regarded as a personal favor.

One or two other people enjoyed the privilege of coming more often. Toni Wolff was, for many years, one of these. Another particularly dear friend of the family who spent much time at Bollingen was Ruth Bailey, an Englishwoman and trained nurse, who had accompanied Jung to Africa when she was young and who came to Switzerland to care for him in his old age. Other friends were sometimes invited if they were passing through Zürich, as well as the occasional prominent personage with whom Jung wished to converse more informally.

During the early years, it was possible to make the 30-kilometer journey from Küsnacht to Bollingen by bicycle, train, or sailboat.[16] Jung had an anchorage there, and he loved to travel via the lake. What is rather surprising is that the Jungs did not acquire a car until 1929. They had not learned to drive and were hesitant at first. Initially, their gardener Muller acted as their chauffeur. Once they realized how much easier life could be thanks to the introduction of this modern means of transport, they actually had two cars. Of the couple, Emma was the first to learn to drive. Equipped with this skill, the journey from Zürich to Bollingen or Schaffhausen was suddenly very simple; it came to constitute a pleasurable outing, and above all it saved a great deal of time.

For a week every summer, starting in 1933, the Jungs and their cohort of faithful followers abandoned Zürich for the shores of Lake Maggiore, where they gathered at a venue close to Locarno and Ascona for the Eranos Tagung. These cosmopolitan, weeklong gatherings were the brainchild of Olga Fröebe-Kapteyn.[17] Held in summer on a large, beautiful property at the edge of a mountain lake, participants were usually able to spend their working days outside on the shaded terraces of Olga's gardens.

During the early years of the Eranos gatherings, the Jungs and other guests stayed at the Hotel Monte Verità close to Olga's villa.

---

16. The two villages have been linked by road and railway for a long time.

17. Olga Fröebe-Kapteyn, of Anglo-Dutch parentage, had attended Hermann Keyserling's School of Wisdom in Darmstadt. Her particular passion was for the different strands of thought from East and West, and in the 1930s she created this exceptional venue for gatherings. Jung had himself met Keyserling, who opined that in Jung he had found the most remarkable mind he had ever met.

Later an apartment was built and reserved for Carl and Emma, who faithfully attended the gatherings for a total of twenty years. During the week of seminars, the paths of the terraced garden overlooking the lake were peopled by dozens of world-famous thinkers and writers from many countries and a wide range of disciplines. A beach was made so that, weather permitting, guests and participants could bathe in the clear waters of the lake. It was, undoubtedly, a welcome form of relaxation for so many brilliant and overheated minds.

Let us mention just a few names to give some idea of the figures who contributed to these gatherings over the years: Mircea Eliade, philosopher and historian of religions; Hermann Hesse, novelist; Heinrich Zimmer, Indologist and specialist in South Asian art; Henry Corbin, an expert on Islam and especially Iran; Karl Kerényi, the eminent connoisseur of the world of mythology; and Wolfgang Pauli, winner of a Nobel Prize in physics. This represented a truly extraordinary gathering of persons and minds, the intersection of so many branches of thought with the freedom to share research findings and ideas, which served the cause of intellectual progress and human understanding. Discussion took place and lectures were given in several languages.

Large numbers of women, pupils or associates of Jung, found themselves transported to Eranos as if by enchantment. Emma was there, naturally, in her capacity as Jung's spouse but above all because of the active role she herself played in the different bodies and associations that had been set up. She contributed to the gatherings by means of her intelligence, her calm presence, and her discretion. Because of these qualities, Emma's company was invariably appreciated and rarely controversial in a setting where, although friendships were apparent, little effort was made to conceal animosities. The participants, however, found the presentations of priceless value for the development of their own work and followed them with both passion and critical intent.

For Jung these gatherings were eagerly awaited and fruitful moments. The intellectually ambitious presentations and interventions enabled him to evaluate his hypotheses, test his intuitions, and obtain feedback on his research through the ideas and comments of specialists from other disciplines. He regarded each separate area of knowledge as essential in its own right and complementary in the search for wholeness of understanding. The construction of his own theories, the concepts and building blocks of analytical psychology, or depth psychology, owed a great deal to all that he heard asserted and debated in this privileged setting. Here Jung presented his own tentative findings. As a researcher he was quite indefatigable, and Eranos represented a true fountain of youth of which under no circumstances did he wish to deprive himself, even if he were feeling tired or sick. During the war years the gatherings were toned down but not discontinued. Most reluctantly, Emma and Carl stopped attending them after 1953 for the event had become too much of a strain on their declining health.

This regular opportunity to take a break from her daily life and family tasks was an occasion for Emma to observe her husband at leisure and to become involved, from a privileged stance, in these intellectual exploits and revelries. Carl's peals of laughter, proof of his pleasure, are legendary. In Eranos he experienced moments of exceptional optimism and freedom. Often the couple would extend the week spent there by taking a mountain holiday in Switzerland or setting out to discover an unknown corner of Italy. Walking together was a form of relaxation that both enjoyed and thus an opportunity for silent and affectionate communion.

Emma sometimes accompanied her husband on his foreign travels, including—in two successive years, 1936 and 1937—trips to the United States. They made the journey on a transatlantic ocean liner. Carl was not at all keen on the social life on board ship but had accepted this choice to please Emma who appreciated the comfort of a luxury cabin and the elegant facilities for relaxation and socialization offered by these floating palaces. Jung's own preference would have been for a slightly longer and less comfortable but more solitary journey on a cargo ship accepting passengers, which would have enabled him to spend his time reading without having to flee from the inevitable requests for interviews.

On the East Coast of the United States the couple received a triumphal welcome. At each of Jung's lectures the auditoriums were packed full. Through the repeated and eloquent enthusiasm of a people so open and receptive to new ideas, events in Maine, Connecticut, New York City, Boston, and at Yale University represented stages in Jung's realization of the extent to which his findings were perceived to be important. This young country, with its rudimentary and unsophisticated notions of psychology and galloping economic progress, was eager to learn. "The psychological problem of today is a spiritual and religious one," Jung was bold enough to tell Americans.

The couple discovered the generous hospitality of several families who, spontaneously and without the least reserve, opened their homes to them. Both Carl and Emma appreciated the wild and unspoiled beauty of the immense open landscapes and national parks that they visited. While Carl was at the center of the discussions, Emma, who attended all the lectures, was able to stand back a bit and observe customs and differences in traditions. The open and surprisingly frank attitudes of the Americans had the effect of putting Emma at ease and enabling her to give expression to a natural vivacity that was often held in check at home in Switzerland among her reserved and frequently mistrustful fellow countrymen and women.

These official journeys served for Emma as ever stronger confirmation that the work accomplished by her husband represented a remarkable feat. She rejoiced in her own good fortune at having a rightful place by his side. In spite of her natural inclination to remain self-effacing and discreet, she was clearly indispensable to Carl. She was there to temper his ill humor and, on occasion, relieve his doubts; she kept a close eye on his wardrobe; she clued him in to certain aspects of the behavior or attitudes of their hosts. Her intelligence in combination with her naturally graceful manner enabled her to behave as an enlightened and reassuring ambassador of her husband's new and astonishing ideas.

It was not until 1948 that Jung himself finally became convinced
of the need to set up an institute. The training of a new generation of
therapists in accordance with the ideas of C. G. Jung could no longer be achieved by the sole means of direct transmission. Jung's ideas
had never really been expressed in terms of establishing a doctrine
or formal teaching. The framework for the practice of therapy, its
content and defining conceptual planks, had never been clearly set
down. Jung had acted as the supreme arbiter and guide, so to speak,
responsible for acknowledging the skills and suitability of any given
disciple wishing to set up as a therapist following the inspiration
contained in his work and teaching. All followers, up to this point,
had passed through his own hands at one moment or another.

Jung was now seventy-three years old and lacked his former energy. His priority at this stage in his life was his writing. His many
disciples were pressing him to give this immense theoretical and
clinical corpus formal shape and recognition. He finally gave in to
the repeated entreaties of Jolande Jacobi and others. The C. G. Jung
Institute was the result of lengthy and close collaboration between
Emma and Carl Jung and some of their closest associates. Their
rather belated and perfectly legitimate concern was to preserve the
originality and particularity of the numerous concepts developed by
the master of depth psychology.

Although Jung agreed to be the first president of the institute, he
soon handed the office over to a close friend, the highly respected
professor Dr. C. A. Meier, himself a psychiatrist and analytical
psychologist. Jung's ambivalence remained, and it was with mixed
feelings that he released his hold on the reins and handed over the
presidency, for it was undeniable that this C. G. Jung Institute was,
in a certain manner, his very own child and the formal testimony to
a life of research and discovery.

Emma, though now age sixty-eight and manifestly weary, agreed
in 1950 to serve as vice president of the newly founded institute. Her
readiness to accept this position appeared all the more remarkable
in that she had already experienced some health problems, of which

she had, however, appeared to make light.[18] Her husband's tacit wish was to see to it that responsibility for ensuring that this new venture ran smoothly along the intended track should be vested in a member of the family.

We can imagine that part of Emma's concern was also to take her own share of the burden represented by creation of the C. G. Jung Institute. The secret shadow areas surrounding their marital difficulties notwithstanding, Emma had never ceased loving her husband; she admired him and felt extremely proud of all that he had accomplished. However, in accepting this position, she chose to put off until later the writing up of her research on the Grail. Jung, in a conversation with Barbara Hannah, expressed his awareness of this consequence and said that he regretted it.

Among her responsibilities, Emma kept a close eye on the teaching and the introduction of evaluation procedures. She also taught the occasional class. Deirdre Bair tells us:

> When students asked questions during the lectures, she treated them as "potential peers" taking careful notes as they spoke before responding to each point raised. If Emma sensed that students were troubled, she found a graceful way to invite them to "come over to the house where they could talk." (Bair 2004, 536)

It is abundantly clear that Emma was viewed by this community with the highest regard. Never was her integrity, her competence, her experience, or her indifference to honors called into question. Since it was first set up, the C. G. Jung Institute has trained thousands of psychologists who come from all over the world to study there. Its official languages were, from the outset, German and English. Zürich, which saw the vital beginnings of this great adventure in psychology, remains to this day an important focus of Jungian endeavors.

---

18. The previous year she had spent two months in the hospital on account of a shoulder fracture resulting from a fall at home.

7

.

Emma and Carl Approaching Old Age

From 1944, the year when Carl was brought to a sudden physical halt with a fractured ankle followed by a heart attack, his own life and the marriage relationship entered a new phase. Emma made the requisite arrangements to enable her to remain constantly at her husband's bedside during the months he spent in the hospital. She successfully established recognition of the distinction between Jung the public figure and Carl the sick patient, even if her insistence in this regard was distasteful to many persons who felt deep admiration and respect for the great man.

There can be no doubt that the severity of the patient's condition was such that he required many weeks of complete rest. Jung's professional life, with its virtually nonstop demands and obligations, had certainly pushed his endurance to its limit. Even before the accident, his physical condition had been undermined and his energy level weakened by the amoeba that had contaminated him during his trip to India.

The Jung children had meanwhile grown to adulthood, and all five now had young families of their own. Although taken up with raising their children, they were naturally prepared, should the need arise, to come to the assistance of their parents. However, Jung, determined to resume his research activities and encouraged by Emma, during the period of his convalescence turned to Marie-Louise von Franz, whom he had first met in 1933 when she was still in her teens. Having subsequently embarked on university studies in the classics and become extremely competent in both Greek and Latin, this young woman agreed to become Jung's research assistant. It was an association that, unlike the earlier collaboration with Toni Wolff, constituted a working relationship devoid of any element of romantic fascination but was nonetheless based on deep mutual respect and affection. For both sides, this was the beginning of a long and highly fruitful working partnership.[19]

The return to normal life was, for both Carl and Emma, very gradual. What becomes all of a sudden apparent at this point, however, is that these two individuals, whose married life we have followed through several decades, were now, according to the standards of the time, an old couple. By the time Carl was well enough to resume his work he had already celebrated his seventieth birthday. Emma, after refusing to allow any form of official celebration but so as not to disappoint his oldest and most loyal friends, had invited the persons closest to Jung to attend a cocktail party held in the garden at Küsnacht immediately before a birthday dinner reserved for family members. As the Jungs' five children had produced a total of nineteen grandchildren, this family celebration was hardly a quiet affair. Emma's surprise birthday gift to her husband, a puppy named Puck, was greatly appreciated and became Jung's faithful companion. Puck filled the void left by their other dogs, all of whom had by now died of old age after a long period during which they had formed an essential part of the Jung family's life.

---

19. Marie-Louise von Franz later became one of the most important of Jung's disciples. After his death, she continued her own outstanding career in a cross-disciplinary area spanning the boundaries between science and psychology. She is one of the writers who did the most to disseminate Jung's ideas. Her books deal, among many other subjects, with the interpretation of fairy tales from the standpoint of Jung's thought as well as her own insights into depth psychology. Marie-Louise von Franz said that she owed everything to Jung. She died in 1998 at the age of eighty-three.

Emma, like Carl, felt an overwhelming need for quiet time to rest, read, write, and simply contemplate her family, the lake, and the garden, whether in Küsnacht or Bollingen. And yet, being a woman of such compassion and so deeply attuned to the concerns of others, she could not resist responding to any manifestation of a need for help. This meant that even though the most appropriate response to her growing weariness might have been to leave Küsnacht for Bollingen, it was by no means rare for Emma to respond to an urgent request by offering a distressed caller a last-minute appointment.

Thus a few more years passed, and we learn from a letter written in 1947—in a tone evocative of Emma's habitual tendency to make light of her problems—that she was forced to go into the hospital for some dental treatment, a health-related disruption that had in actual fact caused her a great deal of pain and discomfort. It was on the day after her treatment that Carl suffered a second heart attack. This time he was not taken to the hospital; arrangements were put in place—though this was hardly straightforward—for him to be cared for at home.

These circumstances had given Jung every opportunity to take full measure of his wife's many qualities. Emma, invariably self-effacing and even-tempered, had seldom thought it fitting to voice her doubts, her feelings of anger, or her unutterable disappointments. It is even reported that, on at least one occasion, Jung spoke to an analysand in praise of his wife, telling the analysand that, whereas many people's character defects become exacerbated in their old age, in his own wife it was quite the opposite: she was possessed of a remarkable personality, extraordinary virtues, and, what is more, was a brilliant student. Nothing, he opined, could provide greater comfort and reassurance than the presence of a woman who remained so exceedingly agreeable into her old age (Cabot Reid 2001, 252).

Those who had known the couple for a long time were touched by the relationship of mutual love and tenderness that became apparent during these later years. By this time relations between Toni Wolff and Jung had taken a more distant turn, enabling some measure of lightheartedness to find its way back into Emma's life. Toni had recently chosen to discontinue her Sunday visits, and, since she had declined to take part in his research on alchemy, Jung no longer lunched with her on Wednesdays.

The year 1950 was to be a time of turning points and new departures. Jung, subject to tremendous inner pressure from the rage to express his ideas, once again became deeply immersed in his writing. This was the reason why he officially resigned from the presidency of the institute. And it was once again out of a feeling of loyalty toward her husband and of respect for the value of his work that Emma agreed to take up a portion of the responsibility that he had laid down.

By this time Jung saw patients only seldom, and when he did, the sessions were usually rather brief. He even announced that he would no longer attend the Eranos gatherings, a decision that represented, for him, a genuine sacrifice.

As he approached his seventy-fifth birthday, Jung reminisced about his own masters—Sigmund Freud, Pierre Janet, Théodore Flournoy, Richard Wilhelm, Heinrich Zimmer, and others—as if compiling a list of those who had accompanied him along his own road to maturity. All these men were now dead.

Throughout her husband's long career, Emma had frequently been present not only as his wife but also as his professional assistant and coworker. At this time, given the state of Carl's health, she took it upon herself to represent him. Thanks to the unmitigated respect that she had always enjoyed, Emma was able to offer those with whom she came into close contact a sense of well-being and a protective and caring atmosphere. This was an attitude that, in a perfectly balanced manner and without in any way imposing herself, expressed Emma's concern for others and thereby contributed to instilling harmony into every kind of situation. The quality on which her patients most frequently remarked in speaking of Emma's analytical skills was her subtlety.

In 1953 Carl and Emma had been married for fifty years. As usual, and in accordance with Emma's express wishes, their golden wedding anniversary was celebrated in the privacy of the family and with a few select friends. It was at this time that the couple made their last journey together, traveling to the Netherlands. For Emma this proved a most enjoyable trip, and she experienced a surge of joy and good humor. Although her own health also sometimes gave cause for concern, Emma was reluctant to pay much attention to it. The children, sensing the vulnerability of their aging parents, showered them both—and their mother in particular—with kindness and affection.

On March 21, 1953, Toni Wolff died suddenly at age sixty-five of a heart attack and stroke, after suffering for many years from serious chronic pain caused by rheumatoid arthritis. She had kept an attentive, albeit discreet, eye on the development of the C. G. Jung Institute, of which she was secretary. The analytical psychology community was shocked and saddened by the news of her death, for Toni had been very closely involved, virtually from the beginning, in this new holistic approach to the health of the psyche. She had been a privileged witness and participant through all the ups and downs of its forty years of growth as well as its most recent new developments. She had been loved and appreciated for her idiosyncratic ways and highly unusual spirit, which had fascinated so many of those who had come into contact with her.

Jung, undoubtedly deeply affected by Toni's death, remained silent and, on the pretext of extreme tiredness, declined to attend her funeral. The stone that he subsequently engraved with the words, vertically arranged, *Toni Wolff Lotus Nun Mysterious* is the only external sign providing any hint of the nature and character of this long intimate relationship. Years later, Jung expressed discreetly to a close friend, Barbara Hannah, the full depth of his gratitude toward Toni. Her presence and her help, he confided, had been invaluable in the years when his psyche had suffered such disturbance during his descent into the most archaic abysses of the individual and collective human unconscious. It was quite impossible that he should forget her.

Emma, too, was touched by Toni's death. Through the refinement of her feeling, she had been enabled to recognize the extent to which the younger woman's presence at Carl's side during his years of inner confrontation had been not only helpful but essential. Evincing her natural compassion, Emma, on observing Toni's deep loneliness, had taken her former rival to some extent under her wing in later years. By this stage in her life Emma had found, so we must believe, a way of transcending her suffering and of accepting the reality of what Carl and Toni had shared.

Toni Wolff's intrusive position in relation to the intimacy of the Jungs' marriage had never been less than glaringly obvious. If during Toni's lifetime people had drawn a respectful veil of silence over what was perfectly apparent, after her death a number of tongues granted themselves the license to comment. In particular, two men who were close to the couple expressed their views on the subject. One of them, Fowler McCormick, remarked that Jung had been lucky to have in Emma a wife who had found a way of tolerating this arrangement, adding that such a relationship constituted an excruciating situation for any wife and had been a torture for Mrs. Jung (Donn 1988, 180). The view expressed by another friend, Joseph Henderson, was that even if Jung had found in two remarkable women two wives, it was an arrangement that could under no circumstances serve as a model, for such a triangular relationship was dependent upon a form of consciousness that utterly transcended the ordinary model of a relationship between a married man and his mistress (Bair 2004, 560).

While Jung had, in practice, succeeded in asserting his right to appear freely in public with his "two wives"—as Emma and Toni had indeed come to be labeled—the situation had been deeply uncomfortable for persons who knew them both and who were fond of Emma and held her in high esteem. While none of these onlookers had the power to offer Emma any help, no one had been able to ignore the many forms of distress and discomfort she had endured on account of this thoroughly untoward arrangement. When in Emma's presence, they could not fail to perceive that her untold dismay at the situation that had befallen her had seeped its way through to the very depths of her soul. Emma, it was remarked, rarely smiled.

Had Emma not been possessed of an iron character, unshakable moral strength, boundless love, and such a finely attuned intelligence, would Carl have been able to rely on her to stand firm and retain her dignity in the face of his own sometimes offensively casual attitude, a manner that was on display for all to witness? Was he not, in this respect, guilty of abusing Emma's love and steadfastness? What price did he pay for his choice to behave in the way he did? What kind of inner torment, what sort of acutely painful split, did his behavior cause him to endure? Is it possible that he was ever delivered, even by death, of this burden of duplicity? The answer to these questions must remain shrouded in mystery, for we are not party to the secrets of the gods.

After the celebration of their golden wedding anniversary, Emma and Carl extended their stay at Bollingen, thanks in part to the efficient help provided by Ruth Bailey, the old family friend who continued to live in England but spent increasingly long periods with the couple, assisting Emma, whose increasing fragility was cause for concern among those close to her, and in particular her husband. Jung, who had been so very sick himself, noticed all of a sudden that his wife, who was seven years younger, was showing clear signs of exhaustion. The illness that led to her death in November 1955 was a cancer that initially developed slowly and then, in the final stage, accelerated its growth.

While Emma herself suspected the diagnosis that would have explained the various symptoms she had been suffering for several months, she kept these suspicions to herself for as long as she could, complaining to no one of her deteriorating health. In May 1955 Jung wrote in a letter that his spare time had been fully taken up by his wife's serious illness. Emma had undergone a successful operation, but her condition remained very weak and she would, he added, require constant nursing care for several weeks.

By July, Emma was well enough to take part in the important festivities organized for Jung's eightieth birthday. Unlike his seventy-fifth birthday, when Emma had succeeded in keeping the celebration a private affair for family and close friends, on this occasion the international Jungian community insisted on contributing to the birthday celebrations, a demand that Emma felt unable to oppose insofar as it is a Swiss tradition to hold public celebrations to mark every fifth birthday after seventy-five.

So on July 25 and 26 a series of celebrations were held to mark the eightieth birthday of the wise man of Küsnacht, this scholar admired and respected by increasingly large numbers of people all over the world. Emma, after her operation and subsequent treatment, was feeling better, and the family was hoping for a remission. Jung, who had doubted whether his wife would be well enough to attend the birthday festivities, appeared in a jubilant state of mind and excellent spirits during these celebrations held to mark what was an important milestone in his own life and that of his family members.

Jung was filled with a sense of awe and wonder as he contemplated the family that he and Emma had together created and by which the two of them were surrounded on this occasion. To a friend, Dr. E. Bennet, he confided how delighted and proud he felt at having brought into being such a large and healthy family consisting of his children, his grandchildren, and his great-grandchildren. For Jung this was a deeply emotional moment; it was, perhaps, as if he felt that a vitally important component of his life was nearing its end. In the course of these celebrations, Emma, to her own and her husband's surprise, received a superb bouquet of flowers in recognition of her personal contribution to her husband's life and work as well as of her own work in the analytical psychology community. This was an occasion on which Emma indeed received a richly deserved ovation and recognition.

Emma survived for another four months, making careful preparations in relation to matters that would affect the lives of those she would shortly leave behind her. Apart from her decision to destroy her correspondence, she paid extreme care to putting her financial affairs in order. Emma had always managed the accounts and paid the bills associated with the overhead entailed by life in such a large house. As confirmed by one of the inheritors of her fortune, Swiss law required that the estate be divided in a specific manner among the surviving husband and the descendants. Emma took all the requisite steps to comply with this requirement. She wished to ensure that her husband would have no financial worries and that her descendants would enjoy the material affluence that she was in a position to bequeath to them.

Emma's exceedingly discreet attitude toward her large fortune undoubtedly served to prevent comment or criticism. She was only too aware of the delicate position she occupied between her own privileged social origins and the growing but complex—and controversial—reputation of her husband, C. G. Jung. It was quite clear that Jung, by this time, had access to sufficient wealth of his own. In this respect at least, Emma had no cause to worry.

On November 21, Jung wrote to a correspondent that he had been very busy since the summer and that his wife was confined to bed suffering from an illness about which he was extremely worried. He nonetheless went on to add extensive commentary on a piece of work that his correspondent had sent him. Then, at the end of the letter, is a brief note dated November 28, in which Jung stated that he could not continue; on the previous day his wife had died after a final acute episode in her illness lasting just five days. In this movingly brief notation, Jung recorded Emma's passing.

Emma died on the morning of November 27, 1955. Her last days included periods of coma interspersed with moments of lucid awareness or sleep brought on by the medication she was given to reduce the pain caused by the metastasis. Both Emma and Carl had been aware of the imminent outcome. Carl had spoken to their doctor, who had supplied unequivocal information concerning the terminal nature of Emma's illness. During her final days and hours Emma was surrounded by her devoted children and grandchildren, for she died at home. Emma Jung, née Rauschenbach, born on March 30, 1882, departed this world four months shy of her seventy-fourth birthday.

The Zürich Psychology Club announced Emma Jung's death and published an obituary stating that Emma, after attending the celebrations on the occasion of her husband's eightieth birthday, had discreetly stepped down from the stage. She had represented the unofficial authority of the Zürich group not because she was Jung's wife but because of her strong and steadfast personality. Of all the women who surrounded Jung, Emma had been the only one who had not been one of his patients, except for a brief analytic relationship at the very beginning of their marriage.

The funeral, which took place at the Küsnacht Temple, where Jung was assisted by his son and sons-in-law, was an intensely emotional and deeply moving ceremony not only for the family but also for the scientific and therapeutic community at the center of which Emma had played such a crucial role. The period of bereavement was for Jung a grueling test, for amid the bewilderment of his grief he gained a new and fuller awareness of the tremendous stability that he had enjoyed thanks to Emma's presence in his life and the cherished companionship that she had provided for almost fifty-three years. In a letter of December 14, 1955, he confided to a correspondent: "After my wife's death I am no longer myself; at my age it is difficult to get over such grief" (Adler 1991, 284).

After Toni's death, Jung had seen to it that her memory was engraved in stone. Overwhelmed by the grief that swept through him during this new period of bereavement, Carl took up his sculptor's chisel, selected a slab of flawless sandstone, and set it against a wall of the tower. Slowly and painstakingly he chiseled in the stone some words and phrases taken from sacred texts that enabled him to honor Emma's memory. Then he sculpted a bowl, giving transparent symbolic expression to all that Emma represented for him.

O VAS INSIGNE DEVOTIONIS ET

OBOEDIENTIAE

DIIS MANIBUS ET GENIO CARISSIMAE

ET FIDISSIMAE UXORIS MEAE EMMA MARIA.

VITAM PEREGIT PASSA MORTUA

LAMENTATA.

EST AETERNITATIS TRANSIVIT IN

MYSTERIUM.

A.MCMLV AET.S.LXXIII

fec et pos. maritus C. G. JUNG 1956[20]

At a complete loss to express with any accuracy the feelings that overwhelmed him whenever he attempted to speak of Emma, Jung repeatedly declared that his wife had been "a queen" or that she was "the foundation stone" of his home. After several months of grief that reduced him to a state of utter lethargy, Jung was finally able to emerge from the pain of bereavement through the mental and physical energy required to engrave the stone.

Ruth Bailey, who, as some readers may be aware, had as a young woman taken part in Jung's expedition to Africa, had remained unmarried. Through all the intervening years she had enjoyed a steady and close relationship with the whole family, who adored Ruth's wit and good humor. She had promised Carl and Emma and their children that she would take care of whichever member of the couple outlived the other, if the surviving member so wished. Ruth, who was of a similar age to the Jung children, understood the dilemma posed for them by their father's future welfare, and it was with considerable relief that the family accepted her offer. It was Ruth, accordingly, who took up the role of Carl Gustav Jung's caregiver and companion for the last years of his life. After his death, she returned

20. "O singular vessel of devotion and obedience to the protective deities and the spirit of my dearest and most faithful wife, Emma Maria, who lived, suffered, died, and whose passing is lamented. She entered the mystery of eternity in the year 1955, age 73 years. Fashioned and put in place by her husband, C. G. Jung in 1956."

to her home country, where she was able to spend the last years of her life in peace and comfort thanks to the infinite gratitude of the Jung children.

The five years during which Jung outlived his wife were, to a significant extent, a period of old age with its chronic ailments and bouts of acute sickness. But they were also a time marked by some important productions which included Jung's "testament," namely, the work entitled *Memories, Dreams, Reflections* that he wrote in collaboration with Aniela Jaffé. Jung also contemplated the meaning of this period during which he survived as a widower. It offered him the opportunity, and indeed the necessity, to ask some questions about the nature of an impersonal family karma and to tackle a number of more personal issues that caused him disquiet or perplexity. Such questions inevitably included his choice of marriage partner and other personal relationships.

There can indeed be little doubt that the particular avenues along which his personal choices had caused his marriage to travel were a subject that weighed heavily on Carl's mind. Emma's fate had been to learn to bear, and to transform, the suffering imposed on her by her husband's betrayal of their marriage commitment. It is quite possible, now that Emma had left the stage, that her departure caused Jung to ponder other questions relating to what might have been— but had failed to be—accomplished in and through this marriage.

That, however, is another story. It is also part of the story of the end of an epoch and the beginning of a long process of evolution and development, through to the present day, attributable to a revolutionary corpus of ideas and original concepts, many of which proved prophetic, and above all to a set of therapeutic tools that can lead any human being who so chooses toward his or her individuation, the conjunction of the opposites, and the realization of the Self.

A constant feature in the development of Emma and Carl Jung's married life was the presence of numerous women. Considerable space has been devoted in our narrative to the crisis situation triggered by Jung's relationship with Sabina Spielrein quite early in his career. The subsequent presence of Toni Wolff within the inner sanctuary of the marriage has also been a central topic. Occasional mention has been made of other women who played a significant role in Carl's and Emma's lives at one time or another. Nadia Néri's *Femmes autour de Jung* will enable any reader who so wishes to learn more about some of them; however, the defining purpose of this book has been to focus essentially upon the life, personality, and experience of Emma Jung.

ᣟ

▪

By Way of Tribute

Having reached the point of paying tribute to Emma Jung, it surely
seems natural to turn to Carl Gustav Jung, who, for better and for
worse and just as he had vowed, spent close to fifty-three years of his
own life with her, from February 4, 1903, until November 27, 1955.

On December 15, 1955, less than three weeks after Emma's death,
Jung wrote to his friend Erich Neumann, who was then living in
Israel:

> Two days before the death of my wife I had what one
> can only call a great illumination which, like a flash of
> lightning, lit up a centuries-old secret that was embodied
> in her and had exerted an unfathomable influence on my
> life. I can only suppose that the illumination came from
> my wife, who was then mostly in a coma, and that the
> tremendous lighting up and release of insight had a retro-
> active effect upon her, and was one reason why she could
> die such a painless and royal death. (Adler 1991, 284)

In *Memories, Dreams, Reflections* Jung describes the visions that
came to him during the period of coma that followed his heart

attack. These visions, he stated, were like emanations from the collective unconscious and appeared as objective images. He went on to write:

> I experienced this objectivity once again later on. That was after the death of my wife. I saw her in a dream which was like a vision. She stood at some distance from me, looking at me squarely. She was in her prime, perhaps about thirty, and wearing the dress which had been made for her many years before by my cousin the medium. It was perhaps the most beautiful thing she had ever worn. Her expression was neither joyful nor sad, but, rather, objectively wise and understanding, without the slightest emotional reaction, as though she were beyond the mist of affects. I knew that it was not she, but a portrait she had made or commissioned for me. It contained the beginning of our relationship, the events of fifty-three years of marriage, and the end of her life also. Face to face with such wholeness one remains speechless, for it can scarcely be comprehended.
>
> The objectivity which I experienced in this dream and in the visions is part of a completed individuation. (Jung 1961, 296)

Finally, the following words spoken by Jung are taken from an interview with Miguel Serrano in Locarno in May 1959, at which time Serrano was the Chilean ambassador to India. Jung had been explaining that "the process of the mystical wedding involves various stages" and went on, says Serrano, "as though he were talking to himself":

> Somewhere there was once a Flower, a Stone, a Crystal, a Queen, a King, a Palace, a Lover, and his Beloved, and this was long ago, on an Island somewhere in the ocean

> five thousand years ago . . . . Such is Love, the Mystic
> Flower of the Soul. This is the centre, the self.

"Jung spoke," Serrano adds, "as though he were in a trance" (McGuire and Hull 1987, 405).

Jung seems to have been referring here to a personal experience of the encounter with his anima. Meanwhile, it is quite possible to imagine that he may have been remembering Emma's love, her irreplaceable presence, her fidelity, and her influence upon him, which was as deep as it had been mysterious.

What is there to add to these avowals of love that spring like a hymn of adoration from the depths of Jung's soul? Here was a man approaching the end of his life on earth; whatever years remained to him were but a reprieve, experienced in the knowledge that death would not be long in extending and tightening its clutch. There can be no doubt that the feelings and experiences that find utterance in these texts are expressions of convictions that provided Jung with a strong existential succor able to transcend the destabilizing effects of conflicts, tremors, doubts, and wanderings. Is he not expressing the extent to which Emma—without necessarily being always aware of it—offered him the unconditional presence that he needed to retain a delicate emotional and mental balance?

Shocked and wounded to the very quick by her passing, he proclaimed the love he had received from one woman, his wife Emma, through the enactment of a mysterious destiny that doubtless owed the seeds and origins of its powerful unfolding to secrets buried deep within the unconscious. It seems perfectly fitting and correct to state here—borrowing Jung's own words—that Emma had indeed, in the highest degree, accomplished her individuation and realized her own Self. It was this achievement that enabled her to form a part of the rock upon which her husband's genius was able to rest and to flourish. Referring to his wife after her death, Jung stated that Emma had been the foundation of his house.

"The development of consciousness is the burden, the suffering, and the blessing of mankind," Jung said in an interview (McGuire and Hull 1987, 248). We may be permitted to share this sentiment and to add that Emma, compelled by the circumstances of a destiny for which she accepted responsibility, underwent the firing process described in the ancient alchemical writings and emerged from this overwhelmingly painful and exacting form of travail transformed and forged anew by the alchemists' fire. The manner in which she had reached this position of awareness and ultimate harmony of being was, beyond any doubt, truly remarkable.

"The growth of consciousness concerning oneself proceeds simultaneously with an awareness of guilt," wrote Emma in her study of the Grail legend, which, as the reader will not have forgotten, had impressed her during her early youth and remained a subject of lifelong engagement (Jung and von Franz 1970, 181). We have every reason to believe that in Emma's own case this imperative to rise up through unconsciousness to consciousness had its roots deep within the very core of her personality. The circumstances of her life acted as a spearhead that pointed the way, compelling her to follow its direction and to ascend through the stages of her difficult path to consciousness. Emma had come to terms with her own excruciatingly painful experience of the tragic aspect of this need for consciousness. She did remain steadfastly committed to the necessity of this encounter as she moved through the stations of her personal route to its attainment. Her commitment and conviction in this respect constitute a deeply moving and inspiring example for others.

9
.

Bringing Together the Strands of the Tapestry

We have taken time to consider different phases and periods in the life of Emma Jung. We have turned the pages of the many chapters through which Emma moved after leaving her hometown of Schaffhausen: her experiences in Zürich, Küsnacht, Ascona, Bollingen, and numerous other destinations. Our account contains references to the relevant historical context and to the social or cultural circumstances of the time. We have mentioned, similarly, some of the important public events and developments that had an impact on Emma's and Carl G. Jung's lives. In the interstices of the epic tale of the life of the great Swiss psychologist Carl Gustav Jung we sought to divine and bring out for the reader the true personality of a remarkable woman.

Now the time has come to draw the strands of our tale together. Recall that we proposed, in the introduction, to compare Emma Rauschenbach Jung's life to a piece of needlework or perhaps a rich tapestry. The body of this work comprises the numerous circumstances that, taken together, make up the seventy-three years of one woman's life. In speaking of the more concrete and external aspects of Emma's life we see how events and situations overlapped and crisscrossed. Against this background are multicolored threads subtly woven into the pattern by Emma herself, according to a personal embroidery that represented her own particular way of giving shape and meaning to the events that formed the framework of her life. These decorative threads provide the means by which we gain access to Emma's inner life and subjective experiences. The resulting fabric is rich in detail, and the strong overall sense is of a complete canvas, even if the fact that many of Emma's secrets remain unrevealed means that not all the motifs can be fully reconstructed.

No one would seriously wish to claim that Emma Jung was devoid of shortcomings, that she did not have her sharp edges, her animosities, her limitations. Such failings, after all, are the stuff of humanity. She would not inspire us today if, in response to the manifold complications of her existence, she had failed to display all the facets of a woman whose lot in life included both wounds and satisfactions, periods of acute suffering interspersed with times of deep happiness.

Emma's particular manner of coping with adversity, of carrying forward her various life tasks and commitments, inspires our respect. Her great strength of character, her sensitivity, her perseverance—all these were powerful weapons in the effort to ensure her survival and continue her development alongside the towering figure of Carl G. Jung. Throughout her struggle, Emma was naturally aware of the immense benefits that she derived from her position as Jung's wife, and she continued to value the turbulent but invariably fascinating life experiences that were the ongoing consequence of her marriage.

Even if the circumstances of her life were decidedly out of the ordinary—not to say privileged—Emma was never a person to adopt airs and graces; she retained, on the contrary, an invariably natural disposition and outlook on life. In contemplating her life we may find inspiration for our own lives. Consideration of the ways that Emma found of coping with difficulty, pain, and complexity can enable us to view in a more creative light the life choices that circumstances might appear to impose upon us. Viewed from such a stance, the figure of Emma may acquire a value that is truly symbolic. Her persistent and sustained endeavors, in any case, indubitably merit our respect.

It is important to realize that Emma was faced with the challenge of inventing her own life along uncharted paths and in the absence of a guide. She was cast directly into the fray of the alternately worshipful friendship and hostile altercations enacted by the two pioneers of psychoanalysis, Sigmund Freud and C. G. Jung. In terms of her own personal knowledge and experience of the development, content, and practice of depth psychology, Emma was far in advance of her time. Knowing as we do that she was an introvert, how can we fail to admire the determination with which she sought personal engagement in the cause of change in the world? She preserved, undeniably, some of the values characteristic of her upbringing in a highly conventional milieu steeped in the traditions of the wealthy Swiss bourgeoisie. Given the presence of a distinctly wild streak in Carl Gustav's character, it is not difficult to perceive in the psychological interplay between the two marriage partners an effect of contrast and complementarity that sometimes tipped over into reciprocal influence. We can be sure, as well, that Emma's traditional values, tried, tested, and fired anew through the perils of righteous rage and radical uncertainty, contributed to keeping her vessel afloat when the storms were at their most tempestuous.

Alongside her discretion and natural reserve, Emma's caring attention to and deep interest in other people was a striking feature of her personality. Her tenacity and determination to overcome difficulties were sustained by her pleasure in learning and need to acquire cultural knowledge and extend the boundaries of her understanding. These qualities represented the natural emanation of a spontaneous curiosity that, as we have seen, had been part of Emma's makeup and outlook from her youth. It was to this propensity in his wife that Jung directed his constant encouragement, urging her to pursue her own path. That advice was based on his frequently repeated conviction that "a marriage which is devoted entirely to mutual understanding is bad for the development of the individual personality" (McGuire and Hull 1987, 402).

What is quite certain is that Emma, from early adulthood, found herself faced with a threefold challenge: to foster a state of balanced well-being within her family, to strive to keep her marriage off the rocks, and with equal determination to pursue her own psychological and personal intellectual development. There can be no doubt that Emma had her work cut out for her. Living in such immediate proximity to the powerful aura of Jung's complex personality, she had to discover within herself the strength that would enable her to maintain her autonomy. Her accomplishment of this lifelong task endowed Emma with maturity and enrichment, as well as with many true joys and satisfactions. Her task was curtailed only by the onset of exhaustion—or perhaps by the grace of deliverance.

The marriage of Emma and Carl G. Jung does not deserve to be set on a pedestal; very much the opposite, perhaps. Yet it can be read by both men and women as a tale yielding a rich harvest of lessons. The experience of these two marriage partners casts light upon the nature of those frequently hidden forces that exert such a powerful weight on the realization of the multifaceted entity that we call marriage. A marriage is composed of two individuals with their own natures and sets of complexes. As such, it presents a truly outstanding challenge, one that Jung himself regarded as particularly delicate and demanding.

The narrative that we have here centered on the person of Emma Jung necessarily acknowledges that this particular marriage was placed under severe strain and threat by the husband's overpowering instinctual drive and the doubts and uncertainties instilled in his wife by his resulting behavior. If their marriage was able to remain on course in spite of repeated episodes of turbulence, it was in important measure thanks to the strength and lovingly steadfast attitude displayed by the wife, but also thanks to her husband's determination to delve ever more deeply into his exploration of the psychological conditions and phenomena at stake. Jung's concern with the life of the human psyche led him to think deeply about and to give expression to many ideas concerning the archetype of the couple and the nature of marriage. It surely cannot be supposed that he failed to examine his own marriage in the light of these considerations. Nor was he himself spared the need to make some crucial and deeply painful personal choices that involved facing up to a number of vital existential questions.

Volume 17 of *The Collected Works of C. G. Jung* includes an essay entitled "Marriage as a Psychological Relationship." The article, in its original form, dates from 1925. It was subsequently incorporated into the volume entitled *The Development of Personality.* Jung writes:

> Regarded as a psychological relationship, marriage is a
> highly complex structure made up of a whole series of
> subjective and objective factors, mostly of a very hetero-
> geneous nature.
>
> . . . .
>
> Seldom or never does a marriage develop into an indi-
> vidual relationship smoothly and without crises. There is
> no birth of consciousness without pain. (Jung 1931)

These statements can throw light upon the perilous and undoubtedly sublime destiny faced by any couple who aspires to true marriage and succeeds in achieving its aim. Symbolically speaking, the couple is a complex and sophisticated alchemical composite. Insofar as it finds ways of resisting the tremors by which it will invariably be assailed, the marriage partnership gradually reveals the holistic beauty which constitutes, potentially, its subtle inner charge. Emma and Carl G. Jung, in the course of more than fifty years of married life, certainly experienced the shock of such transformations.

In approaching the young Emma, Carl Gustav Jung had indubitably been impelled, in a manner that far exceeded all rational considerations, by a combination of unconscious factors, conjunctions, even synchronicities—events not linked by a relationship of cause and effect. The young man, aware of his own modest background, gained access to a position of elevated social standing together with the assurance of a degree of comfort and affluence through the choice of this graceful young upper-class woman as his future wife. He had been won over by the charm of Emma's youthful intelligence and her air of solid self-possession. Carl was able to offer Emma immense wealth in return, in the form of the riches represented by his own mind and passions. Their marriage represented the union, as Jung pointed out, of two different and complementary psychological functions, namely, intuition and sensation.

If Emma Rauschenbach was very much a young girl of her milieu, she had inherited also—from who knows which close or more distant ancestor?—a taste for adventure and enterprise, an attraction to mystery, a need for knowledge and culture. Carl, in winning Emma as his future wife, offered her access to many different openings.

Emma did not default on her marriage vows even if, on a number of occasions, she fell prey to anger, to a sense of deep vulnerability, to extreme solitude. In some measure, she owed this steadfast attitude to values strongly rooted in the culture and traditions in which she had grown up. Yet ultimately, given the obstacles that rose up on her path and given her periods of revolt, despair, and doubt, the source of the strength that she was able to muster was of a distinctly more subtle order and must undoubtedly be sought elsewhere.

A document that possibly testifies to such a source is the text—entitled, in German, "Schuld" and unpublished to date—drafted by Emma in 1916 for a talk she gave at the newly founded Psychology Club in Zürich. *Schuld* can be translated as "fault" or "guilt," or even, in some contexts, as "responsibility." In this talk, Emma, perhaps without being fully aware of it, implicitly shared with her audience her most intimate concern and her deepest torment. What was she to do in this situation imposed upon her by her husband's desire and decision to share his love with another woman? Finding herself totally alone with her dilemma, with this burning and insoluble question, she was forced to turn inward in her need to deal with it. No possible help was to be expected from those around her. It was up to Emma herself to transform this excruciatingly painful situation through her private and personal search and to find a way of endowing it with some kind of meaning. It was necessary to discover a form of original and personal creativity not available from the unsatisfactory traditional answers offered by society to such problems. In seeking a personal response to her situation, Emma resorted to ancient myth, referring to the torments of Prometheus, which were the consequence of his decision to bring fire to mankind. Prometheus, who had dared to oppose Zeus, paid dearly for his insubordination. At the same time, Emma dug deeply into her beloved Grail legend in search of an answer that might help her move forward through the pain. In each instance, it was a question of moving outside and beyond the sphere of collective opinion in order to find her own way, the path of her individuation.

As in the myths of Prometheus and Perceval, Emma was repeatedly and often painfully challenged by her circumstances. The outcome was that she found a way, with the help of these archetypal images, of forging her Self. This encounter with her most intimate energies enabled Emma to develop her eros. She discovered, in this way, the means of transforming passionate love into compassionate—or nonpossessive—love, a feeling that respects the needs of the other but in a way that does not entail sacrifice which would be damaging to her personal integrity. Emma succeeded, gradually, in acquiring the feeling and the certainty that her task, or her vocation, was indeed to accompany Carl, the man she had married and a man who was insatiably and permanently impelled by the power of his genius toward new horizons and the exploration of hitherto unknown spaces.

In Emma's story, we have borrowed from Homer's *Odyssey* to illustrate the subtle and symbolic connections between its mythological figures and our protagonists, Carl and Emma. Penelope emerges as having numerous strong points of kinship with Emma. To keep alive the flame in the hearth, to remain faithful to the love pact, to discourage all other attempts at seduction, such was the mysterious way chosen by Penelope. The faithful wife in the Homeric epic remained silently bent over her loom, intent on ensuring the tight and regular intermeshing of the weft and warp, the symbolic threads that connected and united two human beings. While Odysseus, away in foreign parts, struggled to resist the seductive lure of the fascinations encountered on his voyage, he retained deep within his being the hope of the final union with Penelope, as stressed by Agamemnon's ghost in book 24 of the *Odyssey*:

> Happy Odysseus, how virtuous was the wife you won!
> How single-hearted was your incomparable Penelope,
> how faithfully did she keep remembrance of the husband
> she had wedded! And therefore the fame of her virtue
> will never die, and the Deathless Ones will see to it that
> men on earth have a lovely song in honour of chaste Penelope. (Homer 1980, 290)

In numerous respects and in spite of all their trials and tribulations, it is fitting to recognize in Carl Gustav Jung the yeast that enabled Emma to develop into the woman analyst and writer that she ultimately became. It was Carl's influence and seductive charm that underpinned and sustained Emma's flowering. Thanks to his presence in her life, the flame was kindled, the yeast was activated, the potential for development that lay dormant in Emma's depths was awoken and made manifest for the benefit of those around her as well as for her own personal fulfilment.

The price to be paid was considerable. Destinies such as these are never to be envied. The imperious need to bring to consciousness the contents of the collective unconscious—that ultimately irrepressible dimension of our personal and shared psyche—was the colossal task that fell to C. G. Jung. It is not without good reason that some commentators have seen fit to compare him to a volcano, to a towering mountain, to a giant. To maintain this aberrant voyager of the human psyche within an emotional and mental anchorage and to persevere in subtly fostering a steady relationship of intelligent intimacy was the equally capital task that fell to Emma. There can be little doubt that it was this unceasing effort on her part that enabled Jung to resist the extraordinary pressure of these subterranean forces. Sapping her vitality as it inevitably did, there can be no doubt whatsoever that the task took an exceedingly heavy toll on Emma. The opportunity to depart this life may well have represented a liberation to which her being aspired, a desire perhaps strengthened by the sense and the conviction that she had accomplished her destiny.

Having remained in the shadow of the giant, Emma became, for the author of this narrative, a powerful symbol: a symbol of the air and of the wind, of the breath of the soul which preserves life. Her appearance in my two dreams—of the fish in the well and the magnificent goose—was impressive and yet merely fleeting (p. 4). I took this to be a clear indication that she was not asking for a biography, even less for a hagiography; her request, quite simply, was for a public act of recognition. These symbolic requests were what triggered the urgency to speak about her and all that she represented. As I explored her life, it became clear that she was perceived also as an essentially inner symbol, one that serves as a hearth and container for the accomplishment of a being, a precious crucible composed of stone and of flesh, of intelligence and of love; all of which brings us back to the image and the message engraved by Jung on the memorial stone that he dedicated to Emma one year after her death.

Through many dreams, Emma continued to manifest her presence as I was writing this book. The text message that she left on my mobile phone in another dream before the writing began was unequivocal. It shook me very deeply. In faithfulness to my commitment to offer Emma the recognition she was requesting, it was imperative to pass on her appeal: *"You have to tell them that I suffered deeply."*

What is undeniable is that countless other women could say the same thing. How many such women, in bygone ages and in modern times, have remained faithful to a vocation, to some frequently mysterious vow? How many have shared the destiny of a particular man, a figure to whom they offered their support and encouragement, apparently setting aside any legitimate ambitions or aspirations of their own in order to devote their lives to becoming the spiritual womb and the crucible of his fulfilment?

Is such behavior to be regarded as proof of weakness? Is it a search for glory or for perfection? Should we not see it rather as the manifestation of a gift, of a particular form of talent, of a sacred path through life? Numerous examples of these special and out of the ordinary lives can be called to mind. In many cases they were weighed down by suffering, doubts, or uncertainty; at the same time, they represented a testimony of joy. Can there be any doubt that such lives are archetypal representations of a certain form of womanhood that finds its fulfilment in the experience of supporting a fellow human being in the realization of his or her potential and destiny?

Emma's last photo was taken at Bollingen. It is a portrait of the elderly couple. Emma did not take kindly to being photographed, and in the pictures we have of her she rarely displays a smile. In this snapshot, however, we do see her smiling a smile that is addressed here to her husband Carl and, while suffused with tenderness, is characterized also by a certain detachment. The photo was taken in 1953 or 1954, not long before Emma's death. In it, as she gazes from a short distance at the now aged Carl, she seems to be intimating through her smile that all has now been accomplished. Subjective as such an interpretation may be, the photo does not lack eloquence. Looking back from the present, now that the shadows of a rich and complex life have had time to disperse, it becomes possible to discern the signs of a destiny accomplished. While the pain and suffering of the past have left some deep scars, there is room in the present for an ineffable glow of peaceful acceptance.

Jung, in his memoirs, referred to the likelihood that what could not be accomplished or completed in this world might need to be accomplished or completed on the other side. Can the physical, moral, spiritual, sacred—and perhaps mystical—alliance of a couple be accomplished in all its fullness in this earthly and temporal dimension? Is the couple not urged, perhaps, to move farther along its path to fullness and completion in the mysterious beyond? Might we surmise that a prerequisite for allowing the marriage between Emma and Carl Jung to achieve such fulfilment was that Emma's voice should be heard by us? To ask such a question is to understand that it remains inevitably shrouded in mystery.[21]

This account represents an attempt to respond to Emma's request in a fitting manner. The way in which we have proceeded is to follow Emma herself through the succession of demands and challenges imposed by her destiny. After more than fifty years during which her memory has remained confined within her husband's shadow, it appeared both legitimate and necessary to deliver the other voice of the Jung couple, such that it might gain a fair hearing, which would restore to awareness and memory the full dimension and manifold nuances of the fabric of Emma's life.

Before we conclude this account, two more chapters are required. Their purpose is to take the measure, from closer quarters, of Emma Jung's contribution. The first of these chapters supplies evidence of the place that Emma occupied as a therapist, alongside her husband. After that, we will seek to familiarize the reader, in summarized form, with Emma Jung's writings through a presentation that should bring some insight into the original and personal nature of her thought.

---

21. Numerous other considerations or research projects could be envisaged in the wake of this subject matter. It might well be of interest, for example, to elaborate a general theoretical approach to marriage, or to the psychological experience of women, during the half century between 1900 and 1950.

10

.

Emma Jung as Analyst

Before offering any kind of account of Emma Jung's activity as a psychotherapist, it is essential to establish the nature of the setting in which she undertook and performed this work. Nowadays it may be difficult for us to gain a clear idea of the context in which, during the early part of the twentieth century, the revolution in the field of psychology took place. The wholly new approach to the understanding and treatment of psychopathology set the stage for a series of productions, reversals, rifts, imagined scenarios, and simultaneous developments in numerous directions. Our spontaneous tendency is to project backward onto this stage our current notions in this area, thereby ruling out a proper understanding of what was actually happening.

When Freud and Jung first met in 1907 each of them was in the grip of early enthusiasm for the revolutionary discoveries they so passionately discussed with one another. The two pioneers of the exploration of the unconscious and its boundless mysteries were, above all, avid researchers and experimenters.

Existing ways of seeing disturbances of the psyche were called into question and traditional structures for treatment of the mentally ill were found to be of no help whatsoever. The only tools available to psychiatry were, in many cases, the straitjacket and confinement in an asylum. Hypnosis was one new approach that had been tried out but with somewhat inconclusive results. Innumerable questions were prompted by the phenomena of hysteria, paranoia, and especially psychosis. The new therapeutic approaches opened up numerous paths that were demanding to be explored.

We know what happened to these two pioneers. The consequence of the rift between the two men was the creation of two scientific corpuses and two distinct approaches to an understanding and healing of the human psyche. It is of paramount importance, in this respect, to realize that the half century that led up to World War II was a period of searching, experimentation, and development of new forms of treatment.

Jung, distinguishing his approach to the psyche from Freud's method, which he regarded as somewhat reductionist, emphasized the dimension of human purpose and intent as much as—if not more than—past influences and conditioning. The term *psychoanalysis* came to be used to designate Freud's discoveries exclusively. In order to differentiate and describe his own approach and conception of how the unconscious operates, Jung preferred to speak of "depth psychology" or "analytical psychology."

Freud's principal focus was on describing and treating neurotic disorders. His preferred method of consultation and treatment entailed use of the couch in order to foster the retrieval of long-lost early memories. Jung, initially faced in his hospital work principally with cases of psychosis, sought to understand the collective contents of these patients' disturbed mental condition. On the basis of his discovery that beyond or beneath the personal unconscious there lies an impersonal or collective unconscious, Jung gradually moved away from Freud in his exploration of effective approaches and forms of treatment. Jung's preferred method of treatment involved face-to-face consultation, which suited his highly developed intuition and allowed neutrality to be tempered by genuine empathy. Furthermore, his input as therapist extended, on occasion, to amplifications triggered by and developed in accordance with his patients' dream images and other relevant material.

This brief consideration of attitudes toward healing and therapeutic practices of the time sheds light on Emma Jung and the specific features of her professional development. She was, after all, able to move forward quite naturally as a result of her proximity to Jung and to the therapeutic framework he had devised and which he applied in interactions with the patients who came to him for treatment. What cannot be sufficiently stressed is how unusual and completely atypical Emma's path may appear today in light of the ideas that we currently hold about these matters. Emma Jung, as one of the very first practitioners of analytical psychology, received her training, as did her colleagues and the early assistants, from the founding proponent of this original conception of the human psyche who was none other than her husband Carl Gustav Jung.

We have noted that very early in their marriage Emma was briefly "analyzed" by her husband, who quickly realized that such an undertaking actually made no sense at all. Emma subsequently undertook some more analytical work with Dr. Leonhard Seif, a member of the Burghölzli medical team, who had come to Switzerland from Munich. Freud also acted, on and off, as Emma's "analyst" during the all too short period that their friendship lasted. It is deliberately that we place the terms *analyzed* and *analyst* in quotation marks here, for those who at the time taught or practiced this new form of treatment may be viewed as sorcerer's apprentices originally responsible for gradually conceptualizing the nascent science and techniques that developed into psychoanalysis and analytical psychology as we know these practices today.

It is important, by the same token, to remind the reader that psychoanalytical treatment as practiced today in Western countries bears very limited similarity with the early techniques. We are aware that, even today, the terms of the analytical contract vary significantly from one country to another and from one school of psychotherapy to another. But here we must set aside our knowledge or experience of how things are done nowadays and direct our attention and imagination to the era of the pioneers. Insofar as our particular focus is Emma Jung, this means immersing ourselves in events and developments as they took place during the early twentieth century in Zürich and Küsnacht.

Let us then seek to ascertain the nature of Emma's experience, momentarily discarding all our contemporary prejudices. In the course of this narrative, we have mentioned the professional aspect of Emma's life and development. Here we wish to offer a more detailed description and some explicit assessment of her contribution in this respect. Many people remain quite unaware of the fact—or are extremely surprised to learn—that C. G. Jung's wife was also a talented analyst who, over a long period of time, did much valuable work with her patients.

From the beginning of their marriage and their move into the Burghölzli, Emma actively supported and assisted her husband in his work with his patients, his research, his questions, and his scientific hypotheses. Can any better form of apprenticeship be imagined for approaching, one step at a time, the mysteries of the unconscious and for gaining awareness of its multifaceted manifestations? Carl invariably enjoyed involving Emma in his professional concerns, for she showed a quite spontaneous interest and open-minded curiosity in relation to all the myriad manifestations of the human psyche.

When it came to observing the psychotic manifestations that were on display in this psychiatric setting, Emma Jung had the benefit of occupying a front-row seat. What is more, she was in a position to discuss with Carl—or with other doctors in the vicinity who also worked in close proximity with the patients—whatever happened to be taking place before her eyes.

It is thus that, thanks to her intelligence and innate curiosity, Emma was able to take advantage of what we might describe as an informally conducted, hands-on, in-house training course in psychopathology. It can hardly have been a comfortable setting for a sensitive woman who was at the same time a young wife and mother.

Yet Emma Jung clearly decided to make the most of this learning opportunity as it presented itself to her. Such an attitude on her part is
proof in itself of her great strength of character and her many good
qualities.

In 1914 Emma and Carl G. Jung were already living in Küsnacht
when their fifth child was born, bringing to an end the ten-year period marked by Emma's string of pregnancies. From now on, when
her numerous tasks and responsibilities allowed her a little free time
she resumed her research on the Grail legend. Other areas in which
she developed a particular interest related mainly to mythology but
also the history of religions.

In 1916 Emma, at the age of thirty-four, took on the position of
first president of the Psychology Club in Zürich. This club was the
first official institution to be set up specifically in relation to analytical psychology. Soon after taking up her new position, Emma
offered to this group of early Jungian enthusiasts the lecture entitled
"Schuld." Recalling that Emma, at this time, was faced with the disturbing and deeply painful intrusion of Toni Wolff into her married
life, what she describes in the lecture is the need, in the face of the
difficulties thrown up by life and the essential questions posed by
them, to take one's leave of traditional values, insofar as such values
turn out to be of no help whatsoever in dealing with guilt feelings
and the accompanying sense of responsibility.

In such situations—Emma seems to say—the individual may well
come to realize that it is necessary to consent to a form of sacrifice.
An attitude of resignation or, at the opposite extreme, of anger will
be a source of inner dissatisfaction. Emma was herself facing a dilemma in which she found herself irremediably alone. She had come
to understand that an in-depth transformation of the relationship to
oneself and to the other person, while representing an act that must
indeed be viewed as quasi-unnatural, is nonetheless crucial in such
a situation. Emma's ultimate acceptance that such was indeed the
hard test that she herself faced enabled her to renounce all expecta-
tion of shared love. Reaching deep into her psyche, she discovered

within her own being the wealth of eros. Here she found, simultaneously, the possibility of self-respect, of openness to the other person, of compassion, and of tolerance, and this discovery became for her a source of inner freedom. Eros, thus understood, can almost certainly never be divested of pain. Love is synonymous with interdependence. Eros renounces every vestige of possessiveness, advancing instead hand in hand with progress of the mind, spirit, and soul.

Emma's everyday life was conducted in close proximity to the professional premises in which Carl received his patients. As she frequently managed his appointments, the patients knew her and would sometimes ask for her advice and be happy to receive a more-than-welcome listening ear. Although the different parts of the house were quite separate, the daily life of the family was never very far from the comings and goings up and down the main staircase to Dr. Jung's consulting rooms in the family residence. So it was that Emma—propelled by the exceptional circumstances of the work she had performed on her own psyche, which had allowed her to achieve a decisive inner psychological transformation—took the step of becoming a therapist. In making this transition, she enjoyed her husband's encouragement and full support. He was perfectly aware of his wife's psychological maturity and recognized in her the aptitude and qualities required of an analyst. What is more, such a step was in Jung's own interest.

The practical circumstances that prompted this development were in reality quite simple. Carl, in addition to running his own practice for the benefit of his patients, had taken the time and the trouble to train a few other persons in his ideas and techniques. As the years went by, his workload became ever more excessive. And sometimes he felt the need, or the desire, to spend some time away from home. He also received requests to travel abroad which he did not wish to turn down. On such occasions, he would propose that such and such an analysand—depending on his or her particular need and with his or her agreement—become Emma's or, in other cases, Toni Wolff's patient. Who would dare take issue with this? To start with, everyone thought the world of Emma, who had been from the outset such an active and perceptive member and participant in the analytical psychology circles of Zürich and Küsnacht.

Emma's approach to therapy was inspired by her husband's. It was inspired also by her experience as a woman, a mother, and a researcher. Introverted sensation was Emma's psychological type and constituted, as such, the natural foundation upon which her personality was grounded. Within Jung's psychological typology, sensation is a function based on closeness to the world and to others; it is an approach that is guided not by judgments but by events. It is, as Jung pointed out, an irrational type, one that is, accordingly, directly connected to the unconscious. Persons governed by this fundamental disposition are able to offer a calm presence and an approach characterized by pragmatism. At the same time, Emma's knowledge and skills were the result of her many years spent living with Carl the man and of her almost daily contact with Carl the thinker. Alongside this essential input gained from her husband, Emma's approach represented the fruit of all that she herself had endured and transformed within her own psyche and that had been molded by the resulting personal visions and beliefs.

Emma Jung, in accordance with Carl G. Jung's standard practice, offered her patients face-to-face consultations. This was the preferred technique of the founder of analytical psychology, who knew that all that takes place in the psyche finds expression in the face, that the attitude and movements of the body are valuable pointers such that body language indeed reveals the whole personality, including its disturbances and disorders. The face-to-face mode of therapy transforms the doctor-patient relationship into one of personal empathy and involvement. It is a framework lending itself to the creation of an atmosphere of safety within a situation where the inner forces that are kindled back into life, and which may regain an overwhelming immediacy, can be frequent cause for fear, distress, or dismay.

Emma's consulting room was on the same floor as her husband's but in a different part of their large and spacious residence. Their patients, however, shared the same waiting room on the first floor. Many of those who came were acquainted with one another. Some had previously worked with Jung. Others were in the habit of seeing either Dr. or Mrs. Jung, depending on the circumstances. There were as yet no fixed rules or even traditions in relation to the length or frequency of sessions. In the early days, indeed, it had been Emma who decided on the fee for her husband's consultations because Jung was himself averse to dealing with this aspect of his affairs.

Emma Jung and Toni Wolff, soon joined by Peter Baynes, who had come to Switzerland from England, were the first persons to work as therapists alongside Jung. These three formed the hard core and were, for quite some time, the persons most closely associated with the development and intricacies of their great master's ideas and discoveries. Their own personal contributions were—according to the testimony of patients—complementary and mutually beneficial.

In 1925 when Carl was absent from Küsnacht during the six months of his journey to Africa, not only did Emma take over all the family responsibilities, but she also continued seeing some of the patients whose course of therapy with Jung had been interrupted by his departure.

While such an arrangement may seem exceedingly strange to us today, for the persons concerned it appeared to represent a perfectly natural solution to a problem. There could, after all, be no question of interrupting the treatment of patients who had come from abroad and who planned to stay for only a limited time. And in any case, the defining principles of analytical psychology, whether in relation to normal or pathological manifestations of the psyche, were inspired by the advances made by Jung in combination with the input of his apprentices. Any differences stemming from the personality of the therapist would not adversely affect or undermine the therapeutic process already underway; on the contrary, such differences were likely to provide a facilitating alternative illumination of whatever contents of the psyche were currently being explored.

Depending on the specific situation of the individual who came to consult Dr. Jung, the length and frequency of sessions was variable in the extreme. Arrangements in this respect might depend, for example, on the planned length of a visiting patient's stay or on the need for an emergency consultation; in other cases, arrangements were tailored to the exigencies of an individual patient's long-term quest and exploration in search of the Self. Most of Jung's patients may indeed be said to have been engaged on atypical journeys through life and, in this experimental greenhouse of the psyche, the powerful energy exuded by the famous doctor they had come to consult created a heady and stimulating atmosphere. To this bubbling cauldron, Emma was able to contribute her own partially contrasting qualities of calm attentiveness and quiet solicitude.

Certain aspects relating to formal technique did gradually take shape; the length and frequency of sessions became more established, albeit with room for numerous exceptions. A person arriving from the United States for a three-week stay might see Jung for an inaugural—and sometimes decisive—meeting and, after that, continue in therapy on an almost daily basis with either Emma or Toni. At the end, before returning home, the patient would have another final session with Jung. But whatever else might vary, the stuff of dreams was, and always remained, the core focus and basis of the treatment offered to patients.

Emma Jung—thanks to her sensitivity, her experience, her affinities, and her own knowledge of pain—proved well able to adapt to this particular dynamic. Important testimony to the naturally therapeutic nature of her presence is provided by Peter Baynes. At a time when he was feeling utterly and painfully stuck in an inextricable love triangle, he had the good fortune to spend an evening alone with Emma. The positive outcome of their exchange is described in a letter he wrote to the woman with whom he had fallen in love. This letter is quoted in his biography, and his biographer states that it was Emma Jung, in her own deeply personal and feminine way, who was ultimately able to release Peter from this state of conflict and indecision. He was then able to follow his feeling and go the way that his desire and his own truth were leading him. (Baynes Jansen 2003, 251)

It is a strikingly exceptional occurrence that the wife of one of the pioneers of the revolution in psychology should have played such a central role in crystallizing and developing the therapeutic practices of the new science. Yet this was indeed the role and destiny of Emma Jung, for it is a task that she performed virtually to the end of her life, over a total of approximately thirty-five years.

We are by now well aware that Emma's life was harshly and painfully troubled by the complex marital situation that cast such a dark and lasting shadow over her emotional and family experience. Some sense of consolation for her suffering may be generated by awareness of the remarkable manner in which her endurance of pain became, for Emma, the source of inner transformation, representing a contributory strand to her professional training. These inner experiences, as well as enriching Emma personally, indubitably enhanced her potential for empathy with others, including her patients.

Emma Jung qua analyst was described by her husband as a woman in whom the qualities of the dove were indwelling. By means of this image he paid tribute to the remarkable qualities of her centeredness, her integrity, and her deep generosity of spirit. Invariably, our paths through life impose or propose myriad experiences of pain and suffering, harsh and testing experiences that may have the capacity to engender a transformation of the spirit or the psyche. Emma, for her part, had traversed and explored the length and breadth of her personal labyrinth, devoting her best energies to each of the many stages encountered on the way.

Eros is the tool par excellence. It arises from these manifold developments. It enabled Emma, with a poised accuracy, to inspire her patients in the most fitting and measured sense and made it possible for them to use her presence in seeking a route through their own labyrinths. Emma's knowledge of Greek and Latin opened up for her the doors to the world of mythology. While invaluable in her research activity, this aspect of her knowledge also facilitated the work of dream interpretation represented by amplification, as a means of illuminating and broadening the meaning and understanding of dream language.

Because Emma Jung, the therapist, had come face to face with her own shadow, she was able to face the patient in search of healing openly and without her own projections getting in the way. We have every reason to believe that throughout the many years of her practice as an analyst, Emma constantly enriched and perfected her art. In this respect, and whatever the differences between that early world of analytical psychology and our contemporary attitudes and practices, what was true for Emma remains true today. The preparedness to journey into the depths of the unconscious remains the preliminary and the ongoing work on which the quality of the analytical transference inevitably and necessarily depends.

11

.

Emma Jung as Writer

Reference has been made on several occasions in this book to Emma's writing, and so it is natural, in order to complete our portrait, that we should focus more closely on this aspect of her life and work. The two works by Emma that were published in German and have been translated into English—and other languages—contain her personal development of a number of concepts created and given their original shape by Jung. In the texts written by Emma these concepts are filtered through her own way of seeing and imbued with her personal qualities and her feminine sensitivity. Her contribution to certain ideas of analytical psychology, while bearing a highly original stamp, may at the same time provide for the reader a useful route to familiarization with some concepts relevant to the study and understanding of depth psychology.

The first work is a small book entitled *Animus and Anima*, which contains two separate essays. It was published in German in 1947 when Emma was sixty-five. During the 1930s she had given several talks on the same subject at the Psychology Club. The book was published in an English translation in 1955 and in French in 1981.

The second published work, containing Emma's research on the Grail legend, remained unfinished at her death. This subject, as we have seen, is one that had been of interest to Emma and to which she gave continuing thought during the greater part of her life. There exist other writings, hitherto unpublished, mainly the texts of talks given at the Psychology Club. Their interest being quite evident, it is hoped that permission may be obtained to translate these texts and make them available to the general public in the future.

The two essays contained in *Animus and Anima* are entitled "On the Nature of the Animus" and "The Anima as an Elemental Being." While the anima was a subject extensively explored by Jung in several different texts, less has been written about the animus. It is hardly surprising that Emma should have chosen to take on a pioneering role of tackling this archetype belonging to the female psyche. In so doing, she found it necessary to devise an approach quite different from the one that had been adopted toward the anima, for in numerous respects the problem posed by the animus is quite specific.

The essay begins with some general considerations on the presence of the two archetypal images within the human psyche. Emma reminds the reader that both the animus and the anima constitute archetypes, in other words, a sort of virtual reality common to all humanity that becomes manifest only through the force of emotion. It appears to consciousness in the form of a symbolic representation—an image, a human figure, or even an animal.

The anima is the archetype of the feminine as belonging to a man. It may be said to be a man's "soul." It is the inner component of the complement to his psyche. The anima appears in symbolic form in myths, fairy tales, and legends. It may take the form of a swan, a princess, a witch, a fairy, a goddess, even a sorceress.

Insofar as a woman is naturally intuitive, Emma tells us, she is "especially esteemed, even honoured . . . . If we ask ourselves why second sight and the art of prophecy are ascribed to woman, the answer is that in general she is more open to the unconscious than man" (E. Jung 1957, 54–55).

Emma explains in a clear and straightforward manner that man is called upon to confront this additional personality, which is the inner complement to his outer being. While it is a grave matter to disregard or even stifle this feminine component of his psyche, it is equally important for a man to avoid falling captive to its charms or allowing himself to be dominated by it. The task accordingly is one of taming the anima, holding a dialogue with it, becoming conscious of its nature and presence in a manner that, in the long run, enriches man's psyche, his emotional life, and his relationships, and that above all preserves him from falling prey to unconscious projections. Such projections are liable to cast men into adventures of sometimes fearsome proportions, a risk of which Carl G. Jung had considerable firsthand and painful experience. World literature and drama through the ages are replete with such manifestations of anima fascination.

Jung, significantly, ended up admitting that his own primary psychological function was almost certainly intuition. As such, it is possible to assume, hypothetically, that the attributes of his feminine unconscious, and hence of his anima, were extremely powerful but insufficiently differentiated. The consequence was that they thrust him forward into adventures fueled by his passions. Deprived of the possibility of analyzing his projections, he fell under the spell of the auras of certain women in whom the qualities of the anima were particularly strong and bore affinities with this powerful intuitive component of Jung's own character.

"For a man to take possession of a woman by force is a clear sign that his erotic attitude is at a completely primitive level" (E. Jung 1957, 60). While Emma is referring here to a fairy tale, there can be no doubt that the man whose anima is totally unconscious does indeed have a tendency to grab hold of a woman in the effort to possess her. He then risks alienating his freedom and hers rather than understanding that this is indeed a manifestation of his anima. This means also that if the archetypal force of the anima is not differentiated from the personal projection, the man may fall prey to fascination.

Emma ends her essay on the anima with the following recommendation:

> a man must come to terms with his personal anima, the
> femininity that belongs to him, that accompanies and
> supplements him but may not be allowed to rule him . . . .
> When the anima is recognized and integrated a change of
> attitude occurs towards the feminine generally. (E. Jung
> 1957, 87)

Retrospectively, it is legitimate to believe that Emma herself paid
the high price exacted by the tremendous power of Carl's anima. The
effort to live with this reality demanded all the courage she could
muster. Writing enabled her to gain awareness of the power wielded
by these unconscious processes, which are liable to take hold of us
and cause us to alter our rational behavior.

When Emma comes to tackle the figure of the animus in "On the
Nature of the Animus," she alerts the reader:

> Here I shall attempt to present certain aspects of the an-
> imus without, however, laying claim to a complete com-
> prehension . . . I intend to limit myself here to the ways in
> which the animus appears in its relation to the individual
> and to consciousness. (E. Jung 1957, 2)

The features borne by the animus for a woman are not the same
as those borne by the anima for a man. Rather, the animus seems
to be comparable to a figure who is the bearer of values, either positive or negative, and who inspires the woman or exerts a power of
fascination over her. Such representations, accompanied by feelings,
have a tendency to evolve as the woman develops and, in so doing,
to propose to her a broader vision of her own nature.

The animus figures that appear frequently in dreams can range,
for example, from representations of a wild primitive man to those

of a very wise man or a mystic. These male images correspond to the woman's need for compensation or illumination of her masculine side. The animus thus becomes a partner and the bearer of a new meaning with which her life is to be endowed.

Emma Jung writes:

> The animus image differs in accordance with the woman's particular stage of development or her natural gifts. This image may be transferred to a real man who comes by the animus role because of his resemblance to it; alternatively, it may appear as a dream or phantasy figure; but since it represents a living psychic reality, it lends a definite coloration from within the woman herself to all that she does.
> (E. Jung 1957, 3)

These quotes serve to enlighten us as to the awareness gained by Emma herself and by certain other persons in Jung's immediate circle. This text was written at a time when the position of women in the West entered a remarkable phase of its evolution. Emma Jung may well be regarded as a key figure in this movement, for she felt the need to find a place for herself not only in relation to the man whom she had married but also on the basis of her own personality, interests, plans, and destiny.

To take a woman out of her natural role may in many cases be perceived as a sort of betrayal of her vocation:

> To be sure, the woman does not escape sacrifice. Indeed, for her to become conscious means the giving up of her specifically feminine power. For by her unconsciousness, woman exerts a magical influence on man, a charm that lends her power over him. Because she feels this power instinctively and does not wish to lose it, she often resists to the utmost the process of becoming conscious, even what belongs to the spirit may seem to her extremely

worth striving for. Many women even keep themselves
unconscious solely to avoid making this sacrifice. (E. Jung
1957, 25)

What is at stake here is the need for individuation, which, as Jung
pointed out, is *contra naturam*—a process characterized by the necessity to work *against* nature. This work of individuation virtually
always demands the transgression of collective values as a condition
for achieving one's inner fulfilment.

Emma Jung advocated the need for women to gain consciousness
of their responsibility. A direct fruit of the achievement of such
consciousness is an increased possibility of personal development
and fulfilment. It enables a woman to avoid allowing herself to be
dominated, even possessed, by a negative animus, which may behave capriciously or like a highly spirited horse. Emma Jung states
that "strict and unfailing guidance is needed to control this unstable
directionless spirit, to force it to obey and to work towards a goal"
(E. Jung 1957, 40).

> The problem of the woman of today seems rather to lie
> in her attitude to the animus-logos, to the masculine-
> intellectual element in the narrower sense; because the
> extension of consciousness in general, greater conscious-
> ness in all fields, seems to be an inescapable demand—
> as well as a gift—of our time. (E. Jung 1957, 4)

This essay reveals Emma's wisdom. We may suppose that she was
in her early forties when she embarked on the work that led to the
writing of these two essays. She had at this point already had to find
her own way of coping with several distinct stages of her life as a
woman. She had found herself propelled into a milieu where eman-
cipation of women meant letting go of the social norms and clichés
associated with the values of the conventional bourgeoisie. Encouraged by her husband not to confine herself exclusively within her

role as wife and mother, Emma had harnessed her energy and her creativity for the task of encountering her own animus and, in these essays, she offers us the fruit of her personal investigation. She had indeed found it to be absolutely crucial to conquer and come to grips with her own autonomy.

> The animus can and should help us to gain knowledge and a more impersonal and reasonable way of looking at things. For the woman, with her automatic and oftentimes altogether too subjective sympathy, such an achievement is valuable; . . . above all it makes possible the development of a spiritual attitude which sets us free from the limitation and imprisonment of a narrowly personal standpoint. (E. Jung 1957, 39–40)

It is important to cast our minds and our imagination back to a period and a context in which very few women gained access to those fields of work and professions regarded as essentially masculine. Higher education had been, generally speaking, the preserve of men. But the world that Emma had known in her youth was changing very fast indeed. Her daughters, even though they may not in fact have taken advantage of the opportunity for higher education, already belonged to the transitional generation of young women who were in a better position to claim access to the universities.

In the circles frequented by Carl and Emma, most of the women who developed an interest in analytical psychology were unmarried. As such, they had more time and freedom to cultivate the life of the mind. Emma was one of the very few women within this milieu who was also both a wife and a mother. The psychological work that she was obliged to perform on her conscious psyche in order to extricate herself from her natural role and tasks as wife and mother constituted for Emma a tremendous test of her courage and endurance.

The danger exists for a woman that she may come to identify with her animus and become a sort of virago, characterized by a desiccated and domineering mind that is very much cut off from feeling. Such women are frightening to men and the resulting position of rivalry accentuates in men the need either to run away from such women or to possess them. This situation was a feature of the female microcosm that formed a significant part of the early social and therapeutic universe of analytical psychology.

However, there do exist also several positive unconscious masculine models able to inspire in woman an idea of the value represented for her by her animus. Such models might include, suggests Emma, the figure of a wise man, of an aviator, an explorer, sometimes a man of another race, or a dancer. Each type of ideal figure corresponds to different unconscious representations of a woman's potential which its emergence invites her to bring to consciousness. By cultivating such a model she will be on the way to discovering greater meaning in her own life and to finding the path through life that corresponds to her individual form of being.

The years 1914 to 1940 were crucial years for women in terms of the need to acquire a new dimension beyond that imposed on them by traditional religious and social values. Apart from the industrial and technological developments that led to many new forms of work, World War I sent women into the labor market to replace the men who were away at war and those who never returned from the war. In this way, women discovered their aptitudes and skills and the pleasure of taking responsibility for and performing what had hitherto been regarded as men's tasks. Jung, as we have seen, came into close contact with quite a number of these frequently remarkable women.

What Emma Jung shows us in her essay is that it is important for women to integrate this masculine power in a manner that enables it to be turned into creative activity. The women's liberation movement has not always been animated by an awareness that what is needed is not for women to find ways of dominating men or of striving to be their equal. The imperative need for a woman is to integrate her inner male into her conscious life so as to find for it a specific form of expression in both her personal life and her life in the world.

> Learning to cherish and emphasize feminine values is the primary condition of our holding our own against the masculine principle which is mighty in a double sense— both within the psyche and without. If it attains sole mastery, it threatens that field of woman which is most peculiarly her own, the field in which she can achieve what is most real to her and what she does best—indeed, it endangers her very life. But when women succeed in maintaining themselves against the animus ... it is possible for a woman to be truly a woman in the higher sense, and, at the same time, also being herself, to fulfil her individual human destiny. (E. Jung 1957, 42)

Emma Jung was in a position to witness the evolution of women by observing the women around her. While seeing their potential, she was aware of the temptation experienced by some of them to allow themselves to be consumed by their animus. In her own case, she was faced with the need to combine different vocations and to develop different talents. Though economic and social realities have changed a great deal, Emma's observations and concerns have lost none of their value or interest. They remain of considerable relevance today.

It remains to consider Emma Jung's second published work, *The Grail Legend*, in order to identify a few central themes and tenets that are of particular interest and value because of the ways in which they delineate archetypes. The story of the Holy Grail is an epic tale which still today retains all its freshness and powers of symbolic representation. It is a deeply human drama. The strength of its images is such that the tale addresses our unconscious and our conscious mind, acting as an invitation to readers to see themselves reflected in the narrative as in a mirror.

Emma Jung's enterprise in relation to the Grail legend was a highly ambitious one, for she set out to analyze it not only from a historical but also from a psychological and symbolic standpoint. We may surmise that Emma first became acquainted with this legend as early as 1899, during the year she spent at age seventeen living in Paris with friends of her family; one of the earliest written versions of the legend of the Holy Grail is a work by the twelfth-century French writer Chrétien de Troyes.

Emma began, resumed, continued, and deepened her research on the content of this famous legend during her years as wife, mother, and analyst. She found more free time for this enterprise once her children were more or less grown, after her youngest daughter, Helene, reached the age of eleven. By this time Emma was herself forty-three; it was 1925, and she was to live for another thirty years. Yet her protracted and in-depth study of the Grail legend was not completed by Emma during her lifetime.

Constantly requested, as she was over the years, to give classes or lectures on this particular subject, Emma gave priority to communicating her research findings and ideas to her contemporaries over writing them up for publication. Access to the texts of the original lectures would accordingly be most welcome, for they enable the reader to become acquainted with Emma's style and characteristic energy. Their publication would, for these reasons, be highly desirable.

It was Marie-Louise von Franz who, at C. G. Jung's express request, took over the work on the Grail legend and agreed to complete it after Emma's death, at the same time enriching the foreseen volume with additional relevant research of her own. The bibliography contained in the published work is no less than sixteen pages long, which gives some indication of the extent and complexity of the subject. Von Franz added several completely new chapters as well as developing others through the addition of material of her own. Therefore, the volume as published can be considered to correspond to Emma Jung's original intentions to only a limited extent.

The striking fact that this legend came to interest Emma so deeply at such a young age suggests that it contained a message of very particular importance to her. Though she had not yet gained insight into the world of the unconscious, her intuition had spoken to her in a manner that enabled her to perceive, in this symbolic tale, subject matter relevant to vitally important existential questions and explorations.

When Jung became aware of Emma's interest in the Grail, he readily accepted his wife's intention to conduct in-depth research on the different facets of the legend. He himself made no effort to encroach on this area which she had chosen as her own particular sphere for research. And yet, as becomes evident from acquaintance with the text, the symbolic significance of the Grail quest overlaps to a very considerable extent with other topics and works by C. G. Jung on which he worked during different periods of his life. The numerous references to *Aion*, *Psychology and Alchemy*, and *Mysterium Coniunctionis* prove that the subject taken up by Emma was closely akin to and fully consonant with her husband's ideas and concepts.

The sources of Chrétien de Troyes's version of the Grail legend are found in earlier tales and legends, some of which went back to Celtic times and even to the life of Christ. One such source is the story of Joseph of Arimathea, who is supposed to have collected Christ's blood in a cup after his wounding by the centurion's spear that had pierced his heart. Christ became a symbol of and a model for the Self's realization through sacrifice. This symbol slowly developed in the collective consciousness, and the Middle Ages were a period during which some rich tales evoked this mystery. According to one version of the legend, Joseph, to protect this treasure, carried it to England where it remained hidden for many centuries.

What may be seen to be at stake in this story, symbolically speaking, is the process of individuation. This is a term used by Jung to designate the search consisting in the effort to raise unconscious contents to the level of the conscious mind. It is an endeavor that enables the individual to communicate with the Self, which is the center of each person's individual psyche. The truth, reality, and importance of this claim and endeavor form the core premise of depth psychology.

The symbolic expression of this search for the Self is, accordingly, the proposed grid for a reading and interpretation of the Grail legend in this particular Jungian study. With its wealth of images and archetypal representations, the unconscious concerns evinced by the story of the Holy Grail overlap in many different ways with those of the alchemists, for example. The sequence of stages that characterize the transformation of coarse matter into the alchemists' gold correspond in the Grail legend to the equally subtle and complex quest of the hero traveling in search of the unique and precious object represented by the sacred cup.

This approach to the subject of the Grail legend is summed up by von Franz in the foreword to the book:

> The material provided by the Grail stories will be considered here from the standpoint of C. G. Jung's depth psychology. Like alchemy and its curious symbolic productions, these poetic fantasy creations and their symbolism are also illustrative of deep-seated, unconscious psychic processes that are still of the greatest significance, for they prepare the way to, and anticipate, the religious problem of modern man. (E. Jung and von Franz 1970, 7)

According to Jung, the process of individuation is, for every human being, at the center of the concerns of the life of the unconscious realm of the psyche. It is synonymous with the individual's inner need to achieve her or his unique destiny. The task, in other words, is to seek to encounter one's Self, involving the need to find out for what particular purpose one was born as *this* particular human being and what path one has to forge or to follow in order to accomplish the *opus magnum*.

This *opus magnum* (or "great work") is to bring about the emergence of the energies and forces that dwell in the unconscious and which are, by their very nature, opposed to those of consciousness. These energies constitute the foundation and the fountain of our lives, in all their instinctual, psychic, physical, and spiritual dimensions. When the need to approach these realities is experienced, the aim is to incorporate them into our consciousness and thereby ensure that we do not, unwittingly, allow them to wreak havoc with our lives. The ultimate aim, according to Jung, is to achieve the conjunction of opposites, which allows an expansion of consciousness and a form of genuine communication with the unconscious.

Considered in this way, the religious quest, as described and illustrated in the Grail legend, is characteristic of every human being. It expresses the deep and natural need for connection. The Latin verb *religare* thus refers us to the ontological necessity first to gather together the disparate elements of our conscious being but, above all, to include in them the contents of our unconscious, which will demand expression and take their revenge if they are ignored. This is a fundamentally sacred act.

One of the first images to appear in the Chrétien de Troyes story—the hero of which is named Perceval—is that of the all-powerful and possessive mother who, wanting her son to remain close to her, seeks to prevent him from becoming a man, thus keeping him in a state of unconsciousness. Perceval and his mother live in the forest, this being a symbol of a state of unconsciousness. The boy's father is dead, or in any case out of the picture, so that the child is alone in the face of his destiny.

The call of the Self from within this adolescent boy fortunately proves more powerful than his mother's wishes and efforts to encourage his regression. He becomes fascinated by the tale told by the knights who pass through the forest to explain their quest. The boy sets out to follow them, and this brutal awakening from unconsciousness propels him into the arms of the anima, the archetypal feminine figure by whom he is fascinated.

The inflation that follows this encounter translates into an overweening exaltation in the presence of the mystery that is exerting such a powerful attraction on Perceval. At this point, the boy comes up against his shadow, this "foreign" part of himself that is his unconscious complement but which, because it is in opposition to his conscious image, he has to tame. We learn from the tale that Perceval is so blinded by an omnipotence of the ego that he is unable to receive the message from the king who possesses the secret of the Grail.

Perceval has been given the task of retrieving the spear that wounded the king and of repairing it. This spear symbolizes the need to find the way back to meaning, to something that is right and fitting but that has suffered ill treatment. The king is the bearer of the representation of totality. The Round Table around which he gathers together his knights recalls the table of the Last Supper at which Christ shared bread and wine with his disciples. The symbolism of the king also refers to the notion of sacrifice, of which Christ is the example and, for Western Christianity, the symbol of the Self. Accordingly, success in conjoining the opposites is of necessity accompanied by sacrifice.

"Psychologically, the term 'Self' denotes the psychic totality of the human being which transcends consciousness and underlies the process of individuation and which gradually becomes in the course of this process." This sentence from *The Grail Legend* (98) is actually taken from Jung's work *Aion*. The Grail legend, in other words, depicts and enacts the archetype of the Self, the value of which has been ignored and which has not yet risen to consciousness.

The Middle Ages were a period during which mysticism coexisted with extreme barbarism. The period was characterized also by the importance accorded to courtly love. The figure of woman was respected and sought after for her grace and refinement. As such, this was a time when the anima, by means of projection, occupied a significant place in male psychology, and mystical poems of the period frequently seek to express the mystery of the soul. Emma Jung was undoubtedly sensitive to these expressions.

The Grail—the cup or bowl that received the blood of Christ—is a feminine symbol, a symbol of the soul, of the anima. While it gave birth on the one hand to religious mysticism, it was on the other crassly disregarded and insulted and driven back into the unconscious. The anima thus had to be brought back to consciousness, but this was an operation contrary to nature. The feminine symbolism of the Grail is loaded with meaning and significance. What is represented is a process of compensation triggered in the unconscious and aimed at bringing back to consciousness the fundamental and original need for the feminine to be given back its place as the soul of nature. Nature must accordingly be restored to its position at the heart of life.

The point of this chapter has not been to summarize the book, the subtlety and complexity of which demand a deep and careful reading. There should, however, be no difficulty in understanding why this particular theme and the outcome of this symbolic quest were a subject of such fascination for Emma. The innumerable references in the published book to other traditions or writings prove that Chrétien de Troyes, in writing his unfinished novel *Perceval ou le conte du Graal*, had become fully aware of the deep mystery of this quest and doubtless also of its great value.

That Emma Jung was unable to complete this work for publication is attributable to the infinitely complex and overburdened life that she led, a life that demanded all her energies right up until she breathed her final breath. We may be permitted to believe that Emma Jung, as she approached the end of her life, had realized her individuation to a degree sufficient to enable her to take her leave, without regret, of life on this earth. Her life had contained its riches and its joys, among which she had been destined to contend also with many piercing thorns. The task of redeeming faults is never taken on with impunity, whether the faults be one's own or those committed or suffered by others; such labor inevitably takes its toll on the laborer. That Carl G. Jung considered it important that this work on the Grail should finally be prepared for publication is sufficient indication of the respect he felt for his wife and for her efforts and accomplishments.

12

.

In Fine

Considering her work as an analyst and as a writer, it is clear that Emma Jung's contribution to the life of her time was unique and remarkable. Emma's position as the wife of C. G. Jung was not enough to satisfy her need for personal fulfilment; she experienced the urge to forge a path through life and an identity that would be entirely her own.

Emma succeeded in the formidable challenge of achieving, in relation to her eminent husband, the position of a life partner whose views were heeded and respected. She had the courage of her convictions, was not afraid to voice her opinions, and—if and when necessary—to express disagreement.

Through both her professional work as an analyst and her writing, Emma offered proof of her ability to adopt an independent, nuanced, and critical stance, as well as to influence—in her invariably discreet manner—and even exert authority over those around her.

The subsequent silence that has surrounded her life and destiny prompts some legitimate questions. Emma's own wish—as her descendants invariably stated—was to remain a private person. Why such an assertion? Was it the family's fear that Jung's image might be tarnished if the veil so insistently drawn over the vicissitudes of his married life were to be raised?

The account given in this book springs from the desire to facilitate a broader view of the myriad forms of interaction that took place both within the Jung couple and in Carl's and Emma's engagement with their family and social and professional entourage. In no manner whatsoever is the truly immense value of Jung's thought and teachings called into question; and the psychological truth and reality of the complex experiences that characterized his life will be recognized by countless others who have fallen prey to similarly irresistible passions. Such experience of the psyche is a reality that it is quite pointless to deny and that, as human beings, we ignore at our peril.

A review and reappraisal of what Emma, during her lifetime, had experienced as an outrage was increasingly becoming a necessity. "All the women are in love with him," she had written to Freud as early as 1910 when events had already given her cause to feel uncertain about her position as Jung's wife. Her youngest daughter informs us that her mother was prone to appear assailed by doubts.[22] It had become a matter of urgency to remedy this injustice and to cleanse the wound inflicted upon Emma's womanhood by reflecting upon and placing on record the tremendous challenge she faced and the inner change that she accomplished in meeting it.

During more than one period in the course of their married life Emma truly came to represent a rampart for Carl against the risks and dangers of dissociation. Two specific circumstances may be adduced in support of this claim. The first takes us back to the critical period of Jung's descent into the unconscious during the years 1911 to 1913. The second is the period that followed his heart attack in 1944. Emma stated that her husband was, at times, in the grip of his visions, as if possessed by them. Her own permanent and unconditional presence at his hospital bedside had enabled—or perhaps

---

22. See the testimony of Helene Hoerni-Jung in chapter 5 and in the afterword.

obliged—this man, who in a state of extreme weakness had fallen prey to fascination with the promptings of the unconscious, finally to regain a footing in reality.

In these two specific sets of circumstances Emma provided the symbolic but also physical anchorage that enabled her husband to retain some hold on reality and not to be pitched utterly adrift by the convulsions of a temporarily disordered psyche that placed his life in jeopardy. It is in all likelihood to these very circumstances and dangers that Jung was alluding subsequently when he paid tribute to his wife for the role she had played by his side during some of the most critical times in his life.

Numerous are the situations in which women, experiencing the throes of an unjust, destructive, or simply excruciatingly painful marital situation, either take the decision—quite rightly—to leave or, in their desperation, fall into a state of chronic depression. Emma's choice was to remain with her husband, whom she loved and admired, because she found in her life with him numerous compensations and some forms of true satisfaction.

The most striking features to emerge from this attempt to track some of the important stages on Emma Jung's path are her strength and her inner courage. What we learn from experience is that nothing less than a mysterious and vital necessity, one that springs from the very depths of a person's being, can bring that person face to face with the dark side of his or her personality and being. This is a recognition to which Emma Jung, cast by destiny into the swirling waters of the psychological revolution of her time, did not wish to remain a stranger. Emma bore within her own psyche the signs and openness of disposition and spirit that marked her to become a voyager along such a path.

Following the tortuous paths of the search for the Holy Grail, exploring the symbolism of ancient myths, represented for Emma a route whereby she found she could gain access to her own unconscious reality. These studies opened up to her the doors to an understanding of the great archetypal images.

All of a sudden it is as if these long bygone years can be restored to us today. The light shed by the quality of Emma Jung's being over her married life, her family, and her social and professional milieu seems to be shining once again. If an attempt such as this one to re-infuse Emma's personality and times with life and relevance can prove successful, might it not perhaps be one way of asserting that communication between people alive today and those who lived in the past is able to retain its vitality and pertinence?

Some readers may perhaps object that we have remained too much on our guard in describing Emma Jung's experiences in her family and personal life. Yet we have noted that Emma's own natural mode of being was characterized by deep reserve. In a family context or among friends, it is hard to imagine her succumbing to a temptation to complain openly, to make any kind of emotional outburst, or even to allow others to become privy to her innermost feelings. It was, in many cases, through her writing that Emma found it possible to give some kind of expression to her suffering, her questions, and the process of transformation that she had accepted and undergone.

The powerful aura surrounding Jung scarcely allowed anyone to dream of criticizing him or taking him down from his pedestal. This was the reality with which Emma's day-to-day life was imbued. Within the private space of their marital relations, there can be little doubt that she eloquently proclaimed her suffering, expressing not only her hurt but also her bewilderment and dismay. Her only outlet in the presence of others was recourse to her natural dignity, while in the inner world of her psyche, she faced up to the indispensable need for confrontation and struggle with her unconscious. Today the demands of justice and reparation for ills suffered can well be met without any need to blacken or sanctify one of the marriage partners to the profit or detriment of the other.

You would like me to write about my mother? That's hard for me to do because there's no story to be made out of my mother. She was in no way spectacular; no scandal ever tarnished her image. Her life was marked by no great refusal or sudden breakdown, by temper tantrums or erring from the path, by any tendency to rejoice to the skies or fondness for dicing with death. There is really nothing sensational to report at all.

And so what *was* she like? How did I experience her?

She was calm, understanding, warmhearted, reserved, discreet, rather quiet, introverted, well-balanced, benevolent, peace-loving, circumspect, patient, joyful, humble, clever, well-read, displaying a capacity for objective thought and judgment, intellectually inclined and gifted.

She shared all her husband's interests. In their conversations she was a loyal, lively, yet frequently critical, partner. With strangers she was somewhat inhibited and, in an unfamiliar environment, had a tendency to remain in the background.

To her large household she paid as much attention as was strictly necessary, but housework did not represent her natural bent. While it was important to her to provide good food and a warm and welcoming atmosphere at the family table, her accustomed favorite place was her desk that was to be found in a somewhat dark niche in the large living room where two small windows with colored panes provided just enough dim light to write by. There she would sit, peacefully reading, thinking, or writing. That was also where she studied Greek and Latin and where she sat answering the countless letters received from friends and relations. From that same safe haven she would help us with our homework, benevolently supervise our comings and goings, or urge us to calm down whenever our laughing, games, singing, or dancing became too boisterous. Don't forget that there were five of us children!

Our whole family life was played out in that spacious living room. This included the usually joyful and sometimes turbulent mealtimes, with party meals on special occasions and official meals and conversations with guests who came from near and far. Nor should I forget to mention the two large dogs who were generally to be found under the table and who, all too often, contributed their share to the turbulence.

Father and Mother would play cards with us for hours at a time, even as we grew into adulthood. In the evenings the two of them would sit together playing their complicated games of patience.

With my mother I had—and I'm sure the same is true of my siblings—so many good conversations and discussions, whether over lunch or else seated by the fireplace in the evening. At other times I would spend time alone with her, sometimes in silence, in the seclusion of her office upstairs.

She listened understandingly to our questions and problems. Prohibitions were virtually unheard of. She almost invariably left us to take our own decisions, but not without having first communicated her own views on the matter in hand. We were then free to follow or to disregard her advice. While she was reluctant to tell others what they should do, her moral standards and expectations were clear and well thought through. This was, in most cases, enough to convince us that she was right.

In her writings also, insofar as we had access to them, she struck us as a woman richly endowed with ideas and a talent for argument. Viewed in this light, her occasional bouts of uncertainty appeared all the more surprising.

These are just a few personal impressions and memories of my mother, a feeble attempt to convey her way of being.

What I have not described are the thousand events and happenings of our daily life, and nothing has been said of the countless duties and tasks that it fell to my mother to perform. Nor have I mentioned the endurance and devotion she displayed in the face of the many burdens with which she was forced to contend.

My mother, her calm manner notwithstanding, formed the "infrastructure" of the whole corporate entity that was:

228 Seestrasse.

She exuded a natural authority. This is as much as I can say.

December 2008

Ruth Bailey, 1900–1981

Gret Baumann-Jung, 1906–1995

Ludwig Binswanger, 1881–1966

Eugen Bleuler, 1857–1939

Henry Corbin, 1903–1978

Mircea Eliade, 1907–1986

Théodore Flournoy, 1854–1921

Martha Freud, 1861–1951

Sigmund Freud, 1856–1939

Olga Fröbe-Kapteyn, 1881–1955

Barbara Hannah, 1891–1986

Helene Hoerni-Jung, 1914–2014

Ernst Jakob Homberger, 1869–1955

Marguerite Homberger Rauschenbach, 1883–1969

Jolande Jacobi, 1890–1973

Aniela Jaffé, 1903–1992

Pierre Janet, 1859–1947

Carl Gustav Jung, 1875–1961

Franz Jung, 1908–1996

Karl Kerényi, 1897–1973

Thomas Mann, 1875–1955

Carl Alfred Meier, 1905–1995

Erich Neumann, 1905–1960

Agathe Niehus-Jung, 1904–1998

Marianne Niehus-Jung, 1910–1965

Wolfgang Pauli, 1900–1958

Jean Piaget, 1896–1980

Jean Rauschenbach, 1856–1905

Emma Rauschenbach Jung, 1882–1955

Bertha Rauschenbach Schenk, 1856–1932

Miguel Serrano, 1917–2009

Sabina Spielrein, 1885–1942

Marie-Louise von Franz, 1915–1998

Richard Wilhelm, 1873–1930

Toni Wolff, 1888–1953

Heinrich Zimmer, 1890–1943

Adler, Gerhard, ed. 1991. *C. G. Jung Letters, Volume 2: 1851–1961*. Princeton, NJ: Princeton University Press.

Bair, Deirdre. 2004. *Jung: A Biography*. New York: Back Bay Books.

Baynes Jansen, Diana. 2003. *Jung's Apprentice: A Biography of Helton Godwin Baynes*. Einsiedeln, Switzerland: Daimon Verlag.

Cabot Reid, Jane. 2001. *Jung, My Mother and I*. Einsiedeln, Switzerland: Daimon Verlag.

Carotenuto, Aldo. 1977. *A secret symmetry: Sabina Spielrein between Jung and Freud*. Translated by Arno Pomerans, John Shepley, and Krishna Winston. Reprinted: New York: Pantheon Books, 1982.

Donn, Linda. 1988. *Freud and Jung: Years of Friendship, Years of Loss*. New York: Macmillan.

Hannah, Barbara. 1976. *Jung, His Life and Work: A Biographical Memoir*. New York: Shambhala Publications.

Homer. 1980. *The Odyssey*. Translated by Walter Shewring. London: Oxford University Press.

Jung, Carl Gustav. 1931. "Marriage as a Psychological Relationship." In *The Collected Works of C. G. Jung*, vol. 17, *The Development of Personality*. Princeton, NJ: Princeton University Press, 1954.

Jung, Carl Gustav. 1961. *Memories, Dreams, Reflections*. Recorded and edited by Aniela Jaffé, translated by Richard and Clara Winston. New York: Random House.

Jung, Carl Gustav. 2008. *Children's Dreams 1936–1940*. Princeton, NJ: Princeton University Press.

Jung, Emma. 1957. *Animus and Anima*. Translated by Hildegard Nagel. Zürich: Spring Publications, 1978.

Jung, Emma, and Marie-Louise von Franz. 1970. *The Grail Legend*. Translated by Andrea Dykes. Princeton, NJ: Princeton University Press, 1998.

McGuire, William J., ed. 1974. *The Freud/Jung Letters: The Correspondence between Sigmund Freud and C. G. Jung*. Translated by R. Manheim and R. F. C. Hull. Princeton, NJ: Princeton University Press.

McGuire, W., and R. F. C. Hull. 1987. *C. G. Jung Speaking: Interviews and Encounters*. Princeton, NJ: Princeton University Press.

Néri, Nadia. 2002. *Femmes autour de Jung*. Translated from the Italian by Brigitte Allain-Dupré and Christiane Cesschambre. Paris: Cahiers jungiens de psychanalyse.

Paskauskas, R. Andrew, ed. 1995. *The Complete Correspondence of Sigmund Freud and Ernest Jones 1908–1939*. London: Harvard University Press.

Spielrein, Sabina. 1995. "Destruction as the Cause of Coming into Being." Translated by S. K. Witt. *Psychoanalysis and Contemporary Thought* 18: 85–118. Originally published in 1911.

Additional Resources

Clark-Stern, Elizabeth. 2007. *Out of the Shadows: A Story of Toni Wolff and Emma Jung*. Carmel, CA: Fisher King Press.

Jung, Carl Gustav. 2009. *The Red Book: Liber Novus*. Edited and introduced by Sonu Shamdasani. New York: W. W. Norton.

goose, as symbol, 4
Grail legend, 14, 165–170. *See also* Jung,
  Emma, interest in the legend of the
  Holy Grail
Grail, as a feminine symbol, 170–171
guilt, as a topic explored by Emma
  Jung, 86, 101, 132, 138, 149

Hannah, Barbara, 84, 87, 98, 114, 119
Henderson, Joseph, 120
Hesse, Hermann, 21
  visitor at Küsnacht and
    participant at Eranos, 96, 110
higher education, in Europe in the
  twentieth century, 13, 71–72, 163
Homberger, Ernst Jakob, 28, 30, 69
Homberger, Marguerite Rauschenbach,
  28–29
Homer, *Odyssey* (Homeric epic), 6,
  139–140

individuation, 106, 162, 167–168
inscriptions, on the house in Küsnacht,
  58–59, 89
International Psychoanalytic Congress
  (Weimar, 1911), 35, 42, 51, 53–54, 62

Jacobi, Jolande, 98, 113
Jaffé, Aniela, 126
Janet, Pierre, 18, 118
Jones, Ernest, 51–52
Jones, Florentine Ariosto, 9
Joyce, James, 21
  visitor at Küsnacht, 96
Jung children, 115–116. *See also by
  individual name*
Jung family life, 84
  excursion to Château d'Œx, 90
  move to Küsnacht, 57–59, 96–97
Jung residence, as the locus for the
  Jungs' professional lives, 97–98, 106
Jung, Agathe, 29, 70, 72, 82
Jung, Carl and Emma as a couple
  births of their children, 29–31
  engagement, wedding, and
    honeymoon, 18

golden wedding anniversary,
  119, 121
marital relationship, 44–46,
  54–55, 57, 68, 70, 88, 115, 117,
  126, 136–138, 143, 174, 176
move into the Burghölzli, 21–23
social and professional
  involvement in analytical
  psychology, 93
their hospitality, 103
travels, 111–112, 119
Jung, Carl Gustav
analysis of his wife, 27, 147
and Freud, differences in
  approach, 145–146
at Ölberg, 69
attraction to women, 44–46, 53,
  126–127
bereavement, 124–126, 129–131
birth and death dates, 3
birthdays, 88, 116, 122
break with Freud, 49–55, 59,
  65–66
confrontation with the
  unconscious, 66–67, 69, 72,
  174
demand for reclusion, 71
heart attack and convalescence,
  87–88, 115–118, 129–130, 174
his two wives, 63, 120
his anima or soul, 44, 46, 131,
  159–160
letters to Freud, 40, 45, 58, 61,
  63
like Odysseus, 6, 42, 54, 140
love affair with Sabina Spielrein,
  42–43, 59, 62–63, 101, 127
on marriage, 135–137
passion for sailing and mountain
  excursions, 23–24
polygamous instinct (tendency
  toward infidelity), 44, 46,
  54–55, 57, 63, 77, 126
prevalence of women among his
  followers, 94, 102, 110
prolific correspondent, 104

CPSIA information can be obtained at www.ICGtesting.com
Printed in the USA
BVOW04s0055081214

378289BV00001B/4/P